SACRAMENTO PUBLIC LIBRARY

D0442395

10-26

C

SACRAMENTO, CA 95814

JAN - 1998

The
Seasons of
Rome

ALSO BY PAUL HOFMANN

The Sunny Side of the Alps:
Year-Round Delights in
South Tyrol and the Dolomites

The Spell of the Vienna Woods:
Inspiration and Influence from
Beethoven to Kafka

Switzerland:
The Smart Traveler's Guide to
Zurich, Basel, and Geneva

Roma:
The Smart Traveler's Guide to
the Eternal City

That Fine Italian Hand

Cento Città:
A Guide to the "Hundred Cities &
Towns" of Italy

The Viennese

O Vatican! A Slightly Wicked View
of the Holy See

Rome:
The Sweet, Tempestuous Life

The
Seasons of
Rome

• A Journal •

PAUL HOFMANN

Illustrations by Joanne Morgante

Henry Holt and Company • New York

Henry Holt and Company, Inc.
Publishers since 1866
115 West 18th Street
New York, New York 10011

Henry Holt® is a registered
trademark of Henry Holt and Company, Inc.

Copyright © 1997 by Paul Hofmann
All rights reserved.
Published in Canada by Fitzhenry & Whiteside Ltd.,
195 Allstate Parkway, Markham, Ontario L3R 4T8.

Library of Congress Cataloging-in-Publication Data
Hofmann, Paul.
The seasons of Rome: a journal / Paul Hofmann.
p.   cm.
Includes index.
1. Rome (Italy)—Social life and customs.   2. Rome (Italy)—
Description and travel.   3. Hofmann, Paul—Diaries.
I. Title.
DG807.6.H65   1997   96-10962
914.5′6304929—dc20   CIP

ISBN 0-8050-3890-6

Henry Holt books are available for special
promotions and premiums. For details contact:
Director, Special Markets

First Edition—1997

Designed by Paula R. Szafranski

Printed in the United States of America
All first editions are printed on acid-free paper. ∞

3   5   7   9   10   8   6   4   2

Contents

Contents

Contents

Contents

The Seasons of Rome

Introduction

Everyday Life in a Famous Place

In various intercontinental spots where my former longtime job as a foreign correspondent landed me, there would often be a curfew during spells of trouble. Cooped up at night in a half-empty hotel that the international media representatives had chosen as our temporary headquarters, my colleagues and I would sit around the bar, grousing about our editors at the home office, the local politicos or warlords, greedy cabdrivers, capricious telephones, and the food. Then somebody would inevitably ponder, "Where should one really live if one could choose?"

Our much-traveled and cynical group would always agree there was no Shangri-la, and every apple, big or small, had its worm, yet some locations were surely more desirable as a residence between professional assignments than others. Paris, London, Provence, or

Tuscany were usually mentioned. When I said that I—a native of Vienna and an American citizen—had long established my base in Rome, the reaction was almost always "Lucky you!"

Conversely, when native Romans are angered by yet another transit or sanitation strike, have just had to stand for an hour in an unruly line at the post office to pay their electricity bill, or have had their new car vandalized, they ask me, "You who could move elsewhere, why do you stay in this unlivable city?"

My stock reply is: "I like it here because of the sunshine, the cheap wine, the tender Roman artichokes, the easygoing and humane ways of the Romans, and your *arte di arrangiarsi.*"

This idiomatic phrase is hard to translate. It means that Romans have a knack for "arranging" things, finessing problems, coping with adversity by astute maneuver or simple procrastination, and evading difficulties by ambiguity. It isn't a heroic stance, it can be infuriating to the foreigner, and it isn't *Roman* in the stern sense that the ancients gave to that word. Yet the art of arrangement has enabled its virtuosos to survive all the vicissitudes of a long and at times violent history.

Nothing is as serious as it may seem, is the prevailing Roman attitude toward life today; almost everything can be accommodated. The Romans of our era aren't like the inflexible (and slaveholding) citizens of early republican Rome, as idealized by Polybius and Livy; most of my fellow residents just want to get by. Unpleasant laws are often ignored and thus become inoperative.

Years ago Italy, prodded by its European partners, made it compulsory for motorists and their passengers to fasten seat belts not only on the highways but also in urban areas. Those who didn't had to pay stiff fines—at least for a couple of weeks. Then the rule was forgotten. Today if you see a driver in Rome with his seat belt attached, odds are it is an American tourist in a rented car.

Introduction

If you take into account the fact that present-day Romans attempt to get through their days with a minimum of effort, and you adjust to their good-natured cynicism and mellow customs, you can live tolerably well in this ancient city. Don't betray irritation if somebody is an hour late for an appointment or doesn't show up at all—that's just the way it is here; unexpected punctuality calls for lavish praise. If you try to be friendly, you will win much friendliness in return. Romans are used to foreigners in their midst and will applaud any attempt on their part to speak Italian, however poorly.

One trait that today's Romans value above all is what they call humaneness—compassion for other people's misfortunes, indulgence for someone's failures, a live-and-let-live philosophy, and distaste for vindictiveness. A Roman expression, often invoked after a squabble, is *Volemose bene!* The dialect motto doesn't really mean "Let's love one another!" as a literal translation would suggest, but rather, "Let bygones be bygones, and let's try to get along, everybody!"

One hears a lot of laughter during the Roman day, but the guest or visitor should not insist on finding humor in everything that local people do or say. Many expatriates, tourists and, above all, travel writers seem to think in their patronizing mind-set that it is the role of their hosts to make them laugh all the time— "Come on, be as quaint and humorous as advertised!" Romans, like everybody else, have their share of problems and troubles, even though they are favored by their environment and climate.

That vaunted sunshine, for instance, may be deceptive or excessive at times. We often shiver in underheated apartments in winter, although there is always that glorious day even in January when we can sit outdoors under a cloudless sky, sipping our espresso. Snow visits the city very rarely, and when it does, life on the Seven Hills comes to a standstill for lack of sweeping equipment.

Many among us flee the city during the torrid days in July and August whereas others, including myself, look forward to the hot, lazy summer days in Rome with those two-hour or three-hour siestas and the evenings when the *ponentino* from the nearby Tyrrhenian Sea springs up. We sit in a piazza with a fountain at its center, a flared carafe of blond wine from the nearby hillside on the table, the umbrella pines whispering in the soft westerly breeze.

Sure enough, I miss out on a few things in Rome. No library here even remotely compares with the New York Public Library. Musical life, including the Teatro dell'Opera, is sadly second-class. Most Romans get their intellectual nourishment, such as it is, from television.

On the other hand, I have at least a hundred excellent trattorias to choose from if I want to eat out with friends. We often do so on the spur of the moment—Roman schedules are never tightly structured with appointments penciled in and party time blocked out weeks ahead.

For our kitchens, the bountiful markets provide fresh vegetables and fruits all year, in addition to fish flown in from the Adriatic Sea and Sicily and mozzarella cheese made last night with the milk of the water buffalo bred in the plains near Naples.

There are of course other, less epicurean, reasons why living in Rome can be rewarding. Sigmund Freud suggested in *Civilization and Its Discontents* that the reader should do some fantasizing, imagining a Rome "in which nothing that has once come into existence will have passed away, and all the earlier phases of development continue to exist with the latest one." If you can visualize a city where a third-century B.C. temple filled with togaed worshippers is surrounded by Fiats and motor scooters and topped by a modern satellite dish, you've visualized Rome.

If you look hard enough, Freud's fantasy is real; he himself, a collector of antiquities who nursed ambivalent feelings about Rome, must have been aware of it. Archeology, religion, art, architecture, folkways, and idiom, intermingled and interrelated in this many-layered city, furnish daily proof that the past keeps lingering here. It is equally true, though, that automobiles, soccer, and television are today the dominant passions of a populace that scoffs at scholarly or official rhetoric.

Rhetoric is a Roman affliction. The city has always inspired magniloquence, and often with reason. Already in the epoch of the Punic Wars of the third and second centuries B.C., when the Roman Republic was locked in a life-or-death struggle with Carthage, a woman poet, Melinno, prophesied eternal greatness. In a panegyric in Greek verses she predicted that while Time defeated everybody and everything, Rome alone would "never fall."

When the republic was well on its way toward conquering a far-flung empire, Livy called Rome *caput orbis terrarum*, the center of the world. Temples and altars of the Goddess Rome were built in various countries around the Mediterranean as early as the first century B.C.

Deified Rome was represented in allegorical reliefs and pictures as a young woman seated on military trophies, holding a globe in her hand. The city's name was conveniently associated with the Greek word for strength, *rhomē*, although it was probably derived from the Etruscan name of the Tiber River, *Rumon*. The poets and rhetoricians of the Augustan Age outdid one another in coining high-flown appellations for Rome—the Victorious, the Invincible, and, eventually, *urbs aeterna*, the Eternal City.

Most people in the teeming place were less laudatory, as the ancient satirists attest. Jerry-built houses in the overcrowded city kept collapsing, fires raged through the tenements, and one was likely to be robbed or roughed up if one walked at night without bodyguards. "Honest people are out of place in Rome," the poet Martial complained. But when he at last had left the unlivable city in disgust and returned to his native Bilbilis in Spain, it didn't take long for him to start pining for Rome.

Even in the darkest centuries of the Middle Ages when the city had shrunk to a few thousand people living in isolation amid the ruins of former grandeur while other European capitals excelled in wealth and power, it was still regarded as unique: "Rome's only glory was that she was Rome," the nineteenth-century historian Ferdinand Gregorovius observed.

Fond of turgid declamation, Gregorovius also wrote that "Rome alone among all the cities of the world has been honored with the divine title of Eternal." Our history teacher at the Albertgasse High School in Vienna apparently didn't subscribe to Gregorovius's rhetoric about Rome's uniqueness; one day he asked us to write an essay on the theme "eternal cities," plural. Most of us eleventh graders nominated Jerusalem, Athens, and Rome.

Yet open the French *Encyclopédie,* that 230-year-old monument of the era of Enlightenment, to "Rome," and you find this lapidary definition by the philosophes of proud Paris: "ROME . . . the eternal city . . . still the most famous city in the universe, although the Roman Empire be extinct."

The volume of the *Encyclopédie* containing these exalted words was about to be published in Paris when Edward Gibbon, as he would recall later, "sat musing amidst the ruins of the Capitol" in Rome. Then and there the Englishman first planned to write a *History of the Decline and Fall of the Roman Empire,* "the greatest, perhaps, and most awful scene in the history of mankind."

Introduction

The Rome that inspired Gibbon's stately prose and unsurpassed narrative was a city with a population of 170,000, much smaller than other world centers of the epoch. It wasn't much bigger when Byron hailed it as his "city of the soul." Today Rome numbers three million inhabitants, more than twice as many as in the 1930s when I first saw it.

Having lived in the Italian capital during the last stage of Mussolini's dictatorship, I became exposed to a good deal of chauvinistic rhetoric. *"Roma—Doma!"* ("Rome, dominate!") was a favorite slogan then. I heard it shouted during Blackshirts' parades and saw it painted in large letters on walls. The fascist motto was a ludicrous echo of a famous verse by Virgil: "Be it your concern, Romans, to rule the nations—to spare the conquered and put down the proud."

Rome itself was soon to be ruled by Nazis and dominated by the Gestapo during the German military occupation, 1943/44, and would eventually be liberated by the Allied armies.

After Italy's quick recovery from the disasters of World War II, the name *Rome* became synonymous all over the world with the title of a movie, *La Dolce Vita.* The film depicted an ambiance of beautiful, erotic women and brilliantly decadent men populating the Via Veneto. I worked as a news reporter in the Italian capital off and on during the 1950s but must confess I saw little that resembled the milieu portrayed by the Fellini picture.

Federico Fellini himself admitted that the Via Veneto of his celebrated film had never existed; it was his invention, a grand allegorical fresco. Or a comic strip. Fellini with all his talent and imagination was no Giotto or Luca Signorelli as a frescoist; he had started his career as a cartoonist, freshly arrived in Rome from an Adriatic backwater, Rimini.

Media rhetoric adopted the title of Fellini's film as a cliché that has transformed the "Eternal City" and Byron's "city of the soul" into the imaginary world capital of the Sweet Life.

For most of today's Romans all those titles are meaningless. They still have to pass scholastic tests, find a job, raise a family on an often scanty income, pay rent and bills, cope with traffic anarchy and other big-city challenges, and try to stay healthy in body and mind.

The following journal is a record of how the city and its inhabitants lived through the year from September 1994 to August 1995—prosaically perhaps, but not without relish—as witnessed by a longtime resident. I don't consider myself a Roman by adoption; I am still a foreign observer with my inevitable prejudices, and on occasion I let my thoughts wander back into the city's history and into my personal experiences during half a century in Rome.

September

• Autumn Sting •

As long as I can remember, the Romans have been sneering at City Hall, which occupies one of the most august spots on earth, the Campidoglio or Capitol Hill. Mayors have come and gone, and in the best cases were quickly forgotten; municipal government during the last few decades has been desultory, if not worse. Maybe it is a little better than usual right now, but it's too soon to tell. Today the Campidoglio hardly punctured the lingering summer torpor by announcing new measures to ease traffic woes in the historic urban core, and to raise a little money in the process.

Instead of the sixteen thousand people now permitted to take their cars into the center, as of January 1 only twelve thousand will be admitted. They will have to pay a new $190 annual fee for the privilege of driving into a restricted area where they probably won't find any parking space.

Only hours after the City Hall statement was issued there were the usual protests, but they sounded perfunctory. Most of those at whom the traffic commissioner aimed today's edict are still out of town and will listlessly trickle back during the next few weeks.

When September comes around, Romans expect to be hit with new taxes, tighter regulations, stiffer tariffs, rent increases, and price hikes for anything from a cup of espresso to a box of detergent. It's called the autumn *stangata,* or sting operation, as inevitable and unpleasant as the squally, stifling sirocco wind from Africa that often spoils the tail end of the long Roman summer.

Attempts at curbing urban congestion are nothing new in this ancient city; few things are. Even the traffic commissioners of antiquity, the aediles, banned most chariots and wagons from the districts within the city walls during daytime. Noble and wealthy Romans didn't care: they moved around in litters carried by six or eight slaves, preceded by poor, freeborn hangers-on who, in order to earn their meager handouts, plowed into the milling crowds to open a corridor for their patron who was riding aloft. The fanciest litters were closed and elegantly furnished—the stretch limousines of imperial Rome.

Nights were noisy with the squeaking of wheels, the neighing and mooing of animals, the shouts of coachmen, and the curses of slaves who were unloading bricks, sacks of flour, and other supplies. "It costs a fortune to sleep in the city," moaned Juvenal. He meant a good night's rest required a palace with bedrooms on a quiet patio or a villa surrounded by gardens.

Now, eighteen hundred years later, the car horns, the whining motor scooters and thundering motorcycles, the shouts and laughter from trattorias and café terraces, and the televisions blaring out of open windows until late enliven our nights in the city; the racket is louder in some suburbs than at the center.

But the new fee for the "Centro Storico" (historic center) windshield badge that allows an auto to penetrate the narrow and often crooked streets and the scenic squares in the heart of Rome doesn't apply to the few thousand people who still live in that zone. Among them are some holdouts of the Roman aristocracy still inhabiting parts of their palazzi that haven't yet been sold or rented to fashion ateliers, architects, lawyers, banks, or affluent foreigners. Other residents of the core neighborhoods are hundreds of priests and nuns in their convents, who probably have no cars; janitors and lower-middle-class families; and outright poor people whose landlords haven't yet managed to buy them out or have them evicted.

The historic center of the white windshield signs is an inner-city patch extending from the Pantheon for less than three quarters of a mile in any direction—to the Tiber bend, to the Piazza del Popolo, to the Villa Borghese gardens, and to the Capitol. Of course almost everything in this city and its near and far outskirts is historic soil, yet the Colosseum, for instance, and the Vatican are outside the restricted-traffic zone.

The twelve thousand select people who will be able to drive or be driven into innermost Rome include about a thousand members of the national Parliament; hundreds of high officials, diplomats, and business executives; no fewer than 2,500 journalists and news photographers; and sixteen hundred "others," which means persons with friends in high places. None of the twelve thousand will probably be rattled by an additional $190 a year, an amount that will surely go up in future autumn stings. They will grumble a bit and charge their expense accounts for what it costs to reach the center of Rome in the modern version of the slave-borne litter.

I won't have to shell out the $190, because I have just sold my secondhand "safari brown" BMW. That I got more for it than I spent years ago is an indicator of inflation rather than of a profit from my nursing an automotive antique. I feel liberated, although I liked the mustard-colored car. I got rid of it in order to "simplify, simplify" my non-Thoreauvian life. I no longer have to worry about thieves and vandals, engage in cunning and often frustrated maneuvers to conquer square inches for parking, and pay auto taxes and insurance premiums that rise in ferocious stings year after year. Driving in Rome is no fun anyway, and if I need a car for a trip I head to the rental agency a few blocks from where I live.

Rome, one of the world capitals with the greatest density of motor vehicles in relation to its inhabitants, has 1.8 million registered cars—three for every five residents—and 800,000 motor scooters and motorcycles. During peak hours fully half of all these vehicles are in circulation, but the number of parking slots in the city is, according to official data, only 300,000. Is it surprising that double- and triple-parking has long become a way of life for the harassed Roman motorist? And that the Roman pedestrians, pestered even worse, have to pick their way on sidewalks cluttered with parked two-wheel conveyances that are chained to utility poles, street signs, and the grillwork of buildings as an antitheft precaution? One of the Roman noises that we shall soon hear again day and night is the agonized wailing of auto horns activated by drivers trapped by double-parked cars.

In recent years I had stopped using my BMW for trips to the city center, preferring to walk there in about forty minutes, to take the No. 70 or 64 bus or the subway, or to call a cab. During the last few days, nevertheless, the trusty safari brown car would have come in handy. No municipal police guarded the symbolic road-blocks that are supposed to control vehicular access to the center: it was too hot, traffic was eerily slack all over the semi-deserted city, and most cops were on vacation with the rest of Rome. No parking problem.

Some residents, maybe those who love Rome best, stay in town during August. We savor the relative quiet, the uncluttered piazzas, and the long evenings. One or the other trattoria always stays open for us and for the forlorn tourists, and we linger for hours at the outdoor tables. Going home, we hear water splashing from a nearby fountain.

The summer lull was supposed to have ended yesterday. Since the end of July most stores, espresso bars, and other businesses here have been shuttered; hundreds of signs in every neighborhood proclaimed "Closed Until August 31." Many of these notices were still up today. Miraculously, the sanitation department cleaned up our section this morning, but in other neighborhoods garbage is still piling up.

I felt the lull today as I was waiting for the No. 70 at the bus stop. It wouldn't come. After twenty-five minutes I hailed a taxi that happened to drive by empty. The young cabbie asked where I wanted to go and evidently decided that my city center destination didn't fit into his plans. "Sorry, I need to go to the bathroom," he told me, and drove off.

I would have repaired to the corner espresso shop to do a little more waiting for the No. 70, but its steel grills were forbidding, and its plastic-topped chairs were stacked behind them. I didn't feel like walking in the heat, and a forty-minute wait was eventually rewarded with a nearly empty No. 70 bus, whose driver seemed glad to stop for me.

A friend who lives in the normally crowded Appio section in the city's southeast told me she had been driving for almost an hour in empty streets under a pitiless sun to search for an open pharmacy; she needed a prescription drug for her mother. The one place in her district that (according to the newspaper listings) was supposed to be open today carried a sign reading "Closed because of a death in the family." Perseverance eventually got the cardiac drug for my friend's mother.

She also reported that during the last few weeks she had always found it difficult—impossible on Sundays—to buy fresh milk. "But I can park my new Fiat right in front of our building now," she said.

• The Weather Gods •

SEPTEMBER 4

After two hot and—even for Rome—uncommonly dry months, this afternoon at last brought a thunderstorm and plenty of water. The Romans who had stayed in town had awaited it with growing impatience and, so it seemed, irritation with the weather gods. The temperatures in the city reached 100 degrees Fahrenheit in the torrid afternoons earlier this week as the rains were late. Usually the first downpours break weeks of uninterrupted hot weather here around August 15, the date of Italy's ancient *Ferragosto* festival, which marks the height of the holiday season and empties the capital.

Every year the rains that follow the long summer drought cause emergencies in the city—streets and squares are flooded in a few minutes because the manholes are clogged with all sorts of accumulated debris, water invades basements, and lightning causes power failures. This afternoon's hour-long thunderstorm stuck to the late-summer script. Strong gusts of wind toppled trees and overturned a truck, water rushed down sloping streets and formed pools in intersections, and one of the city's major hospitals was without electricity for twenty minutes. The fire department was swamped with calls, and people who found themselves in the open were drenched in the few seconds it took them to run to the nearest doorway.

But the mood was joyful. A pair of nuns, one of them a young Asian, giggled as they hitched up their skirts to wade across the lagoon that had formed near their combined convent and school, close to where I live. From my windows I enjoyed (that's the right word) the thunderstorm.

I had been quite sure hours earlier, as many other weatherwise Romans must have been, that the rains were coming. We all monitor the winds, which in Rome are very important because they dictate our moods.

Yesterday and all last night the sirocco was blowing, dumping tons of Sahara sand on the city and giving parked cars a blotchy look, as if they had the measles. I woke up with a headache, drank too much coffee, and felt listless—sirocco complaints I share with thousands of other residents. Then the wind turned and came from the west. Aha, I said, This is it! To top things off, the radio reported that heavy rainstorms had come down in Sardinia, the large island west of us that serves as an early-warning weather outpost.

Sure enough, by noon our sky was no longer the glassy azure—typical of sirocco weather—it had been in the morning. Clouds began rolling in from the sea, first bright and high up, then lower and darker.

Just as the initial raindrops were evaporating on our hot terrace, I observed the well-known white helicopter come in from the Alban Hills, make its customary approach in a loop above my head, and descend to the western tip of the Vatican Gardens where the pope's heliport is. John Paul II was returning to the Apostolic Palace from his summer place at Castelgandolfo in the hillside. Did he have advance notice of a weather change? He probably didn't get a signal from Heaven, but maybe the Italian air force, which lends him the helicopter and crew, advised him that radar readings indicated an imminent stormy spell.

The Polish pope and bishop of Rome doesn't like the city's parched summers, it has long transpired; he escapes from the Vatican to his hilltop summer residence (where he had a swimming pool built early in his pontificate) and every year spends a few midsummer weeks high up in the northern Italian Alps. He must have welcomed the *ponente* (west wind), as did all people here to whom I spoke.

Weather watching is nothing new to Rome. In ancient days, when Romans tilled the fields around their village on the Tiber ford and sailed their first boats to the river mouth, they paid much attention to the winds. They tended to personalize the benevolent zephyrs and the violent storms as divinities.

Long before Julius Caesar was born, the wind gods already had their shrine in Rome, the Temple of the *Tempestates*. No trace of it remains, but scholars say it rose at the spot where the United Nations Food and Agriculture Organization (FAO) today has its large white headquarters, south of the Colosseum. The symbolism—food growth depending on climate and weather—was unintentional when that site for the world agency was chosen.

• Gun-Packing Nun •

SEPTEMBER 7

The little Eurocambio storefront office on the Via Francesco Crispi, up from the Spanish Square, where I have been changing dollar bills and checks for at least twenty years, was held up today. The episode would hardly have made a splash were it not for the method the robber chose.

A young nun walked in, said in accented Italian she wasn't feeling well, and asked for a glass of water so she could take a pill. Obligingly, Ivo, one of the two employees, stepped out of his teller's cage, filled a glass with tap water from the washroom, and gave it to the nun. She pulled a gun out of her cowl and hissed: "Give me all the money in that safe!" The safe in the back of the office is visible through the two tellers' windows. Someone had obviously cased the place.

Ivo, a burly man in his fifties who, during his time off, works a vineyard near his home at Albano in the hills south of the city, didn't obey but gripped the woman's wrist to disarm her. She fired and hit him in his right hand; if the shot had landed a few inches to the left she might have killed him. Then, without having got any money, the robber ran out into the street, without her gun, and walked away. The weapon lay on the floor.

The other teller, Paolo, called the police emergency number, 113, to report the incident and request an ambulance. Meanwhile, state police radio cars were alerted to watch out for the gunpacking nun. In a few minutes she was spotted walking in the Via Boncompagni near the Excelsior Hotel and the United States Consulate General, and was detained.

It turned out she was a Brazilian who had also disguised herself as a nun to commit an earlier robbery, which she pulled off successfully. The police had been looking for her ever since she had shown up at a small office of the Banco do Brasil in the Via Ludovisi—in the same neighborhood as Eurocambio—and had received several million lire at gunpoint, far from an exceptional haul but enough to tide her and any possible accomplices over for a few weeks in Rome.

Ivo was fortunate to get off with a flesh wound that required only disinfection and a few stitches and was expected to heal soon. Together with Paolo, he was able to identify the false nun at the police station. "She was no longer dressed as a nun," he told me afterward. "I must say she's quite pretty." He sounded remarkably unresentful, even sympathetic.

The gunwoman told the police interrogators she had held up Eurocambio to get enough money to pay back what she had gotten out of Banco do Brasil: a patriotic refund? The police officers and the two Eurocambio tellers were greatly amused by her explanation.

The Brazilian was escorted in handcuffs to the women's prison in the Via delle Mantellate, near the fetid old Regina Coeli (Queen of Heaven) jail on the right Tiber embankment, where she will be held to await trial on armed robbery charges. The Mantellate prison is a former convent, and some nuns are still taking care of the inmates; the surroundings should be congenial to the Brazilian novice of the Italian correction system.

Ivo and Paolo foresee that she will get away lightly because Italian penal institutions are overcrowded, and that she will be handed over to her home country's authorities and probably will soon be free again. The two tellers didn't seem to mind, but Ivo vowed, "No customer will get a glass of water from me in the future."

The spurious nun is an addition to the large and ever-expanding foreign segment in Rome's prison population. Non-Italian inmates range from Mehmet Ali Ağca, the Turk who attempted to assassinate John Paul II in St. Peter's Square in May 1981, to a motley crowd of drug couriers and peddlers, pickpockets, muggers, robbers, burglars, swindlers, and pimps from various continents. The influx of shady or violent people from abroad is strongest during the Roman tourist season, which stretches from Easter Week to late autumn. The police reckon that the Roman Catholic Church's Holy Year 2000 with its millions of pilgrims will also bring a record invasion of foreign criminals—and probably a few phony nuns, friars, and priests.

• A Dictator Showing Off •

This afternoon I took my wife to the Villa Margherita clinic where she wanted to visit an ailing friend. Since I didn't know the patient well and thought my presence at the bedside might embarrass her, I strolled around the neighborhood during the half hour my wife would be in the sickroom. Passing the Villa Torlonia, I noticed that the neoclassical mansion and its garden pavilions on the Via Nomentana were trussed into steel tubes.

"What's going on here?" I asked a construction worker. He told me that the complex, now owned by the city, had been promised to Rome University, and plenty of structural changes were needed. "We might as well pull down the whole thing and raise a new building."

But of course you don't raze a landmark that goes back to the Renaissance, and which was adorned in the early nineteenth century with a Grecian portico. Rome's 690-year-old university, officially known as La Sapienza (Learning), has as its center a Mussolini-modern campus north of the railroad terminal, but it has institutes and other offshoots in other parts of the city. Faculty and students who will be assigned to the Villa Torlonia outpost of Learning will no doubt love the vast, splendid gardens, which for the last few years have served as a public park.

I walked around, looking for the red-clay tennis court that I remembered so well, but I couldn't find it. Yet it was there when I first set foot in the Villa Torlonia gardens more than fifty years ago; Mussolini was showing off on it.

At the sidelines then were a group of foreign journalists, I among them. I was a newcomer to Rome. In my native Vienna I had worked as a student for a Swiss newspaper, *Berner Tagblatt*, and my status as correspondent of a foreign publication enabled me to get an exit visa after Austria had become a province of Hitler's Greater Germany. I emigrated to Italy and joined the Foreign Press Association in Rome, where I soon found myself to be part of a group of international journalists invited to Mussolini's private residence, the Villa Torlonia. We thought we were going to get an interview with Il Duce, but his idea of press relations was different.

Mussolini and his family had been living in the mansion since 1925 and had exclusive use of the gardens. Police were posted all around the walled property day and night. The estate was one of several Rome possessions of the fabulously rich Prince Torlonia, who was glad and honored that the dictator had consented to be his tenant, rent-free of course.

The Torlonias belonged to the "black" aristocracy, meaning that their forebears had served the papacy, and their first loyalty was to the Vatican. However, such old, proud "black" clans as the Chigis, Colonnas, and Orsinis, who had produced cardinals and popes and had once wielded enormous power in Rome, snubbed Mussolini's landlord as an upstart. He was a descendant of a banker from Siena, Giovanni Raimondo Torlonia, who a little more than a century earlier had arranged loans for the pope, done other services for the church, and bought himself princely estates and the titles that went with them.

When my new colleagues of the Foreign Press Association and I, some twenty persons, had cleared the police controls at the iron gate of the Villa Torlonia walls, we were astonished not to be admitted into the main building. Instead, we were escorted to a tennis court and told to stand at one side and wait. It was early in the afternoon, and the sun was strong. After a little while Il Duce appeared, followed by a young man, both in whites. I was struck by how short Mussolini was; in the pictures that the Italian newspapers published almost daily he looked much taller. When he was photographed at the side of the runty King Victor Emmanuel III, the dictator seemed to tower over the sovereign.

Mussolini didn't deign to look at us, and started playing tennis with the young fellow who had come with him. The official who had led us to the sidelines whispered that the partner of Il Duce was a champion of the Fascist Tennis Federation.

After a few practice shots the couple played two sets, the younger man making every effort to lose. For his fifty-six years of age, Il Duce moved vigorously and proved he could get the ball back over the net if it was aimed at him.

A twenty-minute display of his tennis skills seemed sufficient to the dictator; he walked toward us and had each of us presented to him by our escort. Mussolini acknowledged each name and the mention of the publications that we represented with a curt nod. Of course there were no handshakes; fascists didn't shake hands but greeted with their right arm stretched out, though on that occasion Mussolini didn't give us the fascist salute, either.

Then Il Duce said all of six words—in German: *"Bin ich krank? Bin ich müde?"* (Am I sick? Am I tired?). The Nazi correspondents in our group, delighted to hear the master of Italy use their language, dutifully guffawed and shook their heads in demonstrative incredulity as if flabbergasted that anyone should suggest such an enormity. Whereupon Il Duce gave us another nod and stalked off.

That's what it was all about, I said to myself. Newspapers and broadcasts in Britain and the United States had reported that

Mussolini was depressed, fatigued, and ailing. His performance on the clay court was intended to disprove such assertions and to reassure Hitler and the Nazi leadership that he was in top form.

Since my arrival in Rome I too had heard of Mussolini's health troubles. An old stomach ulcer was said to have been acting up again, and there were also more sinister rumors. Actually, on the tennis court Il Duce looked sallow rather than tanned. The correspondent of *Neue Zürcher Zeitung*, Switzerland's most important daily, who was an old-timer in Rome, said to me afterward: "Did you notice? With all the heat and exertion he didn't perspire, not even under his arms. A sure sign of liver disease." Whatever was wrong with the dictator, we would later learn that it wasn't hepatitis or any other liver condition.

During Mussolini's grandstanding I glimpsed two heads in a window of the mansion—members of his family or police guards? Il Duce was living at the Villa Torlonia with his wife, the earthy and resolute Donna Rachele, and four of their children; their eldest daughter, Edda, had moved out when she married Count Galeazzo Ciano, who at the time of that tennis game was Italy's foreign minister.

Even I, a greenhorn in Rome, had already learned from my new Italian friends that Mussolini was keeping a quasi-official mistress, Claretta Petacci, on the side. It was not widely known, though, at the time that she had the use of a small apartment in the Palazzo Venezia, the dictator's official headquarters, and spent many hours every day there, waiting for his attentions.

In the evening, every evening, Il Duce came home to the Villa Torlonia. Romans who passed the Piazza Venezia late at night nevertheless saw lights in the windows of his study near the balcony from which he used to harangue the crowds. He left the lights burning to suggest that the sleepless ruler of Italy was still at work for the nation's welfare and greatness.

Actually, the dictator needed his eight or even nine hours of sleep and was probably already in bed if he didn't watch an after-dinner film in his private movie theater in the Villa Torlonia. Stan Laurel and Oliver Hardy were his favorites.

That performance on the tennis court was one of the very few times any outsiders were allowed to penetrate Mussolini's private residence. He never cared for parties, and when he had to entertain official guests he would generally ask them to some government building.

The Italian press didn't print a word about the afternoon show in the Villa Torlonia to which Il Duce had treated foreign journalists. Almost three years later he left the mansion one July morning to report to the king. Rachele, his wife, had ominous forebodings and urged him not to go, somewhat as Shakespeare's Calphurnia entreated Julius Caesar: "You shall not stir out of your house today."

Mussolini, who had always identified with Caesar, did go and never came back, nor did he ever see his longtime home again. Victor Emmanuel III didn't have him murdered, but he was arrested.

The deposed dictator was first held on an island, then in a winter sports hotel seven thousand feet up on the Gran Sasso d'Italia in the Abruzzi Mountains. A German airborne commando freed him, and at Hitler's request Mussolini proclaimed a Fascist "Social Republic." This pro-Nazi phantom state never controlled more than northern Italy and kept shrinking as the Allied troops advanced from the south. Communist partisans captured Mussolini and Claretta Petacci on Lake Como and shot them in April 1945.

When I first walked into the Villa Torlonia gardens and watched the dictator's prowess with the tennis racket, I didn't know that vast Jewish catacombs were below us. Mussolini, however, must have been aware that his residence was sitting on a system of galleries and tomb chambers in which Jewish families had buried their dead in the second and third centuries A.D.

The subterranean corridors cut into soft rock extend over five miles; they had first been explored in the nineteenth century. Other underground Jewish cemeteries are along the ancient Appian Way close to the Christian catacombs; many Jewish tombs are engraved with menorahs and marked with inscriptions in Latin, Greek, Aramaic, and Hebrew. Because of cave-ins, the catacombs below the Villa Torlonia cannot be visited at present.

Today, when I picked up my wife at the clinic, she asked me what I had been doing. "I wandered into my distant past," I told her, "and it seemed like yesterday."

• Parliamentarians at the Pantheon •

When Massimo—or as I should write, The Honorable Massimo, since my friend of ten years is now a member of the Chamber of Deputies—called to say we should get together, I asked where. "Anywhere around the Pantheon would be fine," he said. The two-thousand-year-old temple is about halfway between the two houses of Parliament, the Chamber and the Senate, and the many eating places in the narrow streets and on the squares all around swarm with legislators at lunch and dinner.

Would Fortunato's be okay? "Too establishment," Massimo objected. Fortunato's was the almost official Socialist Party hangout when that moderately left-wing force, under Premier Bettino Craxi, was a powerful political machine. Then Craxi was disgraced, and his party fell to pieces in the corruption scandals of the early 1990s, causing a steep decline in Fortunato's fortunes. Yet the well-run trattoria, true to its auspicious name, recouped quickly. Its three rooms are now filled at mealtimes with lawmakers of what Italians call their Second Republic. Massimo, one of the freshman deputies, must have been there more than once, and appeared to prefer a less conspicuous place for lunch and a chat.

We settled on Armando's on the other side of the Piazza della Rotonda (which most Romans call Piazza del Pantheon). I made the reservation and was there first. When Massimo entered, the mustachioed owner, who had given me a routine greeting, welcomed him with a loud and deferential *"Buon giorno, onorevole!"* My friend didn't seem to mind that he had been recognized as an honorable member of Parliament. I soon learned that he isn't doing too badly in the capital for a northerner who has been sneering at Rome and the Romans as long as I have known him.

During his campaign last spring, Massimo, an architect, kept blasting the Roman bureaucracy as corrupt, wasteful, lazy, and inefficient, and denounced Italy's Deep South as a bottomless barrel into which northern tax money was forever being poured with Roman connivance.

"Gnocchi, of course," Massimo replied to the waiter's question as to what he wanted for starters. It was Thursday, and my friend, the militant northerner, knew that in Rome since time immemorial this is the day for the small dumplings that should be shaped by hand of potato dough rather than machine-made of pasta flour. At Armando's the gnocchi were of the authentic potato kind. Playing the old Roman, I asked Massimo, "What's the correct dish on Fridays?" *"Baccalà,"* he said. *Baccalà* is codfish, and his answer was correct. "What about Saturday?" I continued the test. *"Trippa,"* Massimo replied unerringly. I personally am not a partisan of tripe, but most genuine Romans love it and expect to get it at their favorite trattoria on Saturday.

I tried not to make too much of my friend's new culinary expertise but was pleasantly surprised. I had first met Massimo during a vacation in the Alps, and over the years we had eaten many risottos in various Milan restaurants whenever I visited that city. He had rarely come to Rome. We were friends the way many people are in Italy: He never asked me to his home on the outskirts of Milan, and I had met his wife only during that mountain vacation long ago. We would call each other from time to time to ask for information on various matters or to chat.

Massimo built villas, supermarkets, and small industrial plants in Lombardy; he clearly liked what he did and was well off. I was astonished when he told me somewhat sheepishly that he had been talked into running for Parliament. When he was elected, I sent him a congratulatory fax.

Now, over the gnocchi and the subsequent veal course, Massimo reported on his experiences as a Chamber of Deputies freshman and part-time Rome resident. He had taken a room at the Colonna Palace Hotel, which faces the Chamber building, but he found that too many of his new colleagues had had the same idea. "We run into one another all the time, at breakfast, at the bar, in the elevator and in the corridors, it's like boarding school or army barracks," he told me.

To get more privacy, my friend was looking for a small furnished apartment, and that search was one of the reasons why he had wanted to see me. Alas, I said, to find such a pad at an affordable rent in Rome isn't easy at all. Landlords prefer to let apartments as offices rather than for residential purposes because rent control doesn't apply to offices. "You'll find plenty of so-called offices in nice neighborhoods," I advised. "Have a look at a few, and you will often find there is at least a couch for spending the night, and also a kitchenette or full-fledged kitchen to make yourself breakfast or light meals if you like. The landlord won't object as long as the fiction is maintained that the place is your office, not your living quarters. Or change the rent laws—you are a legislator, aren't you?"

Massimo said that as an out-of-town deputy he was getting a lodging allowance; he would tell his administrative assistant, also paid by Parliament, to seek a suitable "office."

"She is really a niece of mine," my friend confided. "I hired her mainly to answer my mail; she is in her third year studying law at Rome University, and it's a big favor for my sister and brother-in-law. Anna doesn't have to carry my briefcase." Massimo was alluding to the Roman political jargon *portaborse* (briefcase carrier), denoting hangers-on of lawmakers. Quite a few of the young people who habitually carry the bulky attaché cases of senators and deputies become involved in politics, establish contacts with lobbyists, bureaucrats, and favor seekers, and may eventually attain influential positions in their own right. If their patron wins the chairmanship of some parliamentary committee or a government post, they will get an official job or may handle public relations.

Massimo doesn't seem to count on political advancement. He shuttles every weekend between Rome and Milan by air—not so much to take care of his constituents, it seems, as to look after his own business. He says he will probably become a full-time architect again after the end of the current legislature instead of running for another Chamber term.

My friend appears to savor the prestige and the many privileges of life as a lawmaker, however, and not to mind the bustle of parliamentary life. In the morning, he tells me, he gets up much later than he would in the north—"nothing happens in Rome before ten A.M. anyway." After reading the political stories of the major newspapers, he crosses the square between his hotel and Montecitorio Palace, the seat of the Chamber.

As Massimo approaches the portal, the military sentries posted left and right present arms. They of course didn't recognize the legislator from the north, because the soldiers change daily in a rotation pattern giving the army, navy, and air force a chance to pay respect to Parliament; but a Chamber employee who discreetly hovers near the sentries had whispered *"onorevole!"* to alert them that they had to spring to attention. The soldiers don't have to salute journalists or other nondeputies who happen to walk through the main entrance, yet sometimes they do so by mistake.

Once inside Montecitorio Palace, the *onorevoli* are well taken care of. For each of the 620 representatives of the Italian people there are two Chamber employees, many of whom in their black uniforms are deferential as butlers, though a tad condescending toward newcomers like Massimo. The Montecitorio staff are generously paid, better than other government workers at comparable levels.

Massimo himself, after serving only one term, will be entitled to a lifetime state pension higher than what a teacher or middle-echelon official gets after thirty-five years.

For the deputies, Montecitorio Palace provides special amenities—a banking window, a post office, free telephones, and a large library, among other things. Many legislators, especially southerners, first make a beeline for the parliamentary barbershop for an inexpensive shave and facial. Massimo instead heads for the rows of deputies' mailboxes to empty his own.

After sifting the day's mail and assigning her day's work to Anna, his assistant who has by now shown up, Massimo proceeds to the morning's central event: cappuccino in the Transatlantico. This is a large, rectangular hall with settees along the wood-paneled walls. When it was opened in a newly built annex to the three-hundred-year-old Montecitorio Palace early in this century, the sumptuous corridor-cum-coffee-bar outside the vast hall for plenary meetings suggested to legislators and journalists the splendor of the transatlantic liners that were then sailing between Genoa and New York.

Since then the Transatlantico has been a forum for political deal making and intrigue. Deputies consistently slip out of plenary or committee meetings to get yet another cup of coffee or a snack at the Transatlantico bar (at special low prices) or to walk up and down with a colleague to plot parliamentary strategy. Or they may allow themselves to be drawn into a corner by a reporter and, seemingly unaware of what they are doing, engineer a political leak or float a rumor.

Political reporters and some columnists are admitted to the Chamber building, as are the administrative assistants of deputies, including my friend's niece. Much of the real legislative work is done in the committees rather than in the plenary sessions with their oratory and roll calls. Like other members, Massimo has learned to do some reading, draft letters, or write speeches of his own when colleagues drone on in boring debates.

If my friend has no lunch engagement—as he had with me today—he patronizes the Chamber cafeteria which, he reports, serves good and inexpensive food. It too is accessible to parliamentary reporters if there is enough space. Table talk is usually political gossip, according to Massimo, although on Mondays the subject is soccer.

Evenings, Massimo always eats out or goes to some party—"I've never had such a social life back home." I gather that his wife is getting jealous, and that he calls her every night when he is in Rome to set her mind at rest. She hasn't yet visited him in the capital.

Massimo and I, while getting through our gnocchi and our basil-flavored veal, have drunk a liter carafe of Armando's straw-colored Frascati. We skip dessert. I walk my friend back to his hotel and—before I can suggest it—he stops at Tazza d'Oro. That coffee-bean roaster and espresso bar a few steps from the Pantheon brews what many Romans swear is the best coffee in town. "Quite a discovery!" Massimo says naively. For decades I, like many other residents, have made long detours for a cappuccino at Tazza d'Oro.

I leave my honorable friend at his hotel and suggest to him, What about a siesta? "Yeah," he says, "I think I'll have a little nap. You know, I never do it at home, but neither do I drink half a liter of wine at lunch there. To tell the truth, I have become rather addicted to that afternoon snooze, also because nothing is going on until five P.M. anyway." Massimo, the dynamic northerner, appears well on his way toward becoming Romanized, I sense, yet I don't tell him. I am not so sure he won't try to hold on to his Chamber seat when the current legislature ends.

Walking back to a belated little siesta of my own, I pass Giolitti's on the Via degli Uffici del Vicario, a few steps left of the main portal of Montecitorio Palace. The old, renowned establishment, now resplendent with marble, travertine, chromium, and neon lights, is filled with people, and all the metal chairs around the tables outside on the narrow street are taken. I recognize quite a few *onorevoli* of left-wing and right-wing parties, chatting amiably. Some of the patrons sip espresso, but most lick at gelato cones or spoon whipped cream and gelato out of glasses and metal cups; Giolitti's is famous for its gelato. It's also known as the Chamber's antechamber because of massive patronage by deputies.

The sign above the entrance still reads "Latteria Giolitti," identifying the place as a milk shop, although few customers now ask for milk. When I first came to know Giolitti's, it was still essentially a dairy business the way Giuseppe Giolitti—the great-grandfather of the present owner—had started it in 1890. Whenever I came for cappuccino, which I did often, maids and children of families who were then still living in the neighborhood kept dropping in all the time to ask for a liter or two of milk to take home. In summer, it is true, kids would get gelato cones at Giolitti's. There were only two flavors, vanilla and chocolate; at present there are two dozen. One of the countermen now is an Egyptian. Next time I speak to Massimo I must ask him whether he has "discovered" Giolitti's.

• School, at Last •

SEPTEMBER 19

The academic year started for elementary and high school students today—later than in almost any other European country, and a week later than in northern Italy. At Rome's three state universities and other institutions of higher learning classes won't begin before mid-October. Long, hot summers and the city's easygoing ways have always conspired to give young scholars and their teachers plenty of time off.

Just when the school doors opened this morning a heavy thunderstorm came down. The usual floods in some streets and squares, traffic jams, and arguments in many families resulted. "I won't send you to school, Pamela!" said a mother in a loud voice into the open door behind her from the balcony facing our kitchen, after appraising the pelting rain. Seven-year-old Pamela, whom I have known since she was a baby, is burdened, like hundreds of other Roman girls of her age, with a foreign name that an imported soap opera made fashionable in Italy at the time of her birth. It is pronounced Pa-MAY-lah here because that's the way the Italian-dubbed version of the American serial rendered it. A few seconds later Pamela's father stepped out onto the balcony for meteorological observation of his own, and shouted into the room behind him, "You are going! I'll take you with the car right to the school entrance!"

I don't know whether Pamela did attend the first day in her elementary school class; at any rate, because of the rainstorm and the thousands of parents driving their children to school, there was near-paralysis in the streets. I talked to another student, Eugenio, who manfully strode to his mother's small car in front of our building but found time in our lobby to confide to me with a grin, "I hate school!"

Eugenio flunked math and Latin last spring, and his father (a marchese, or marquis, no less) had to pay for tutors all summer to drum enough knowledge into the boy's head (currently adorned by the latest teenage hairstyle—a little pigtail) to enable him to pass the "reparative examinations" before the new school year. Somehow, Eugenio made it. The marchese, with whom I often exchange a few words, told me: "The kid isn't dumb but lazy, lazy! He spoiled his own vacation and ours, and it cost a lot of money." The marchese isn't rich; both he and his wife work for a living, and tutoring isn't cheap.

Eugenio was probably in the last batch of failing high school students to be given another chance without having to repeat a grade. The education minister just announced that, beginning next year, there won't be any "reparative" tests. If the authorities follow through with the threat, which many people still don't take seriously, thousands of Roman high school students who failed end-of-term exams would have untroubled, though glum, vacations, and many teachers and other persons who pick up some money in summer by tutoring would lose that source of income, although they might recoup it during the academic year.

The announced abolition of the "reparative examinations" is part of proposed education reform legislation that would also extend mandatory schooling from fourteen years of age, as it is now, to sixteen. Furthermore, students would have to learn not just one foreign language but two. English is, unsurprisingly, the foreign language favored by most parents and students; however, it is not available in some schools right now. Teachers of French, German, or Spanish, on the other hand, are underemployed.

By stretching compulsory schooling to sixteen years of age, the government would provide jobs for many teachers who otherwise would be unemployed because there aren't enough students. Italy has the lowest birth rate in Europe, and the city of the popes would rank high in a championship of contraception. Scores of classes in the city's schools are again being abolished this semester.

Early this afternoon when the rains had subsided I passed the Mamiani High School, a large, dirt-yellow complex on the broad, straight, tree-lined Viale Giulio Cesare, just after the students had been dismissed from their first class. The school's walls had been cleaned during the summer, but new graffiti have already appeared. One reads "Fight With Us!" though it doesn't say who "us" is or what the fight is supposed to be about.

Fifty or so students, male and female, were still milling in front of Mamiani High in some sort of uniform of their own—blue jeans, leather or jean jackets, running shoes or clunky footwear. Virtually everyone carried a multicolored INVICTA backpack; that brand, which comes in various models, has been the correct school equipment for years, a triumph of advertising and peer pressure.

Several students unlocked heavy chains with which they had fastened their motor scooters to gates or stanchions; they must have ridden on those conveyances during the morning downpour. One fellow, probably a senior and a big man at Mamiani High, drove off on a Japanese motorcycle with a petite faux-blonde on the pillion.

I know what will happen later this afternoon. Hundreds of students of Mamiani High and other schools will crowd into the Maraldi bookstore opposite the Vatican walls to buy the textbooks that their teachers told them they will need. Maraldi's is a favorite because it has a well-stocked secondhand books section. Many of the used textbooks in it, however, have become obsolete because teachers all too often prescribe new revised editions or entirely new titles. Is there a split-fee conspiracy between faculties and publishers? That has often been alleged, and it wouldn't cause much surprise if it proved true. Schools don't provide textbooks but expect parents to shell out the money for them. To the marchese in my building that will cost another three hundred dollars or so.

• Bulldozers •

SEPTEMBER 27

According to state radio reports, bulldozers sent by City Hall arrived this morning at a cluster of semi-completed buildings on the far northern outskirts of Rome and started wrecking them. "Why us?" wailed the owners of the four structures that were to become units of an unlicensed housing project, which calls itself Flaminia Garden Cooperative. "Construction without official building permits is going on all around this area, and many of the projects are much bigger than ours," they claimed.

"We have to start somewhere," City Hall responded. To demolish unfinished buildings is much easier under Italian law than those that are roofed and already inhabited. The problem is aggravated by the circumstance that the four little villas of the Flaminia Garden rose on an archeological site. The Etruscan city of Veii flourished there when Rome was nothing but a struggling settlement of fishermen and farmers.

The ancient sophistication of Veii is impressively documented by many artifacts unearthed in the area, now on display in collections in Italy and abroad. Most famous among them is a life-size painted terra-cotta statue, known as the Apollo of Veii, in the Etruscan Museum in Rome's Villa Giulia; the bronze sculpture of the Roman She-Wolf on the Capitol is also believed to have come from Veii.

I first explored the ruined walls, arches, tufa caves, and ramparts of Veii one Sunday soon after I became a Rome resident. With me were three Spanish journalist colleagues, one of whom, Luis Gonzales Alonso, was also a teacher and the most erudite of the four of us. In a nearby trattoria overlooking a ravine, Don Luis lectured us on the Etruscans' fundamental contributions to Roman civilization. "They taught the Romans how to build an arch, how to grow wine, and how to tend olive trees," I remember him telling us over carafes of rough wine.

The countryside around the little village of Veio near the Etruscan ruins, which we had reached on rented bicycles, was then solitary. Today Rome is grasping it along two branches of the Via Cassia (National Highway No. 2) and along the Via Flaminia (National Highway No. 3). Suburban housing and other constructions are lining the highways and spreading between them. Most of the new buildings have gone up illegally, but so far the authorities have rarely attempted to undo this blatant violation of zoning rules.

Today I called Alberto, a pioneer of wildcat real estate development, to ask him about the city action against Flaminia Garden. "They didn't pay off the right people," he said with a chuckle. "At any rate, we here are now okay," he smugly assured me. Alberto is chairman of a cooperative that, without bothering to apply for building permits (which would have been denied), has so far erected housing units for two hundred families west of the Via Cassia.

Over the phone Alberto explained that his cooperative had struck a deal with City Hall whereby its new cluster of houses located in what was once a lonely stretch of rolling sheep pastures was declared legal after the cooperative had promised to pay a sum specified by installments. The transaction was made possible by the latest *condono*, or legal pardon, that the national Parliament has just enacted. By now it's a cherished institution: periodically, the Italian state tacitly admits it is powerless to curb the chaotic property development that is going on throughout the country, especially in metropolitan areas and along the coasts, and takes advantage of it to at least raise additional funds for the ever-hungry Treasury.

I have known Alberto many years, long before he took early retirement from his job as driver-messenger in a publishing firm to devote his uncommon talents as a smooth operator to his cooperative full-time. I never truly enjoyed the few trips I had with Alberto in his company's big Alfa Romeo. He was a reckless driver, took hair-raising risks in Rome's traffic free-for-all, and was inconsiderate toward pedestrians. Surprisingly, as far as I know he never had an accident.

Alberto's real estate career started when, after long litigation, he and his family were evicted from a suburban apartment for which he had been paying a ridiculously low rent. The family had to move to another, much more expensive, place; Alberto decided to build his own house.

I don't know how he financed the purchase of a plot of pasture, ostensibly for sheep farming, some ten miles north of Rome's center. I suppose he borrowed the money—it can't have been very much—from peasant relatives in his native Umbria.

Alberto, a short, prematurely gray fellow fond of malapropisms, revealed considerable stubbornness and cunning in his real estate ventures. He immediately started breaking ground for a house on his tract of land, which by the city's zoning map was dedicated to "agricultural purposes." Of course he had no building permit.

He hired workmen and, pitching in himself on his days off, managed to raise a provisional structure that was really no more than a basement. Once or twice during the preliminary work municipal policemen showed up at the site, but Alberto "persuaded the cops to leave me alone," as he confided to me with a conspiratorial smirk.

His basement had no water supply, sewerage, or electricity, but Alberto and his family moved in anyway, and they roughed it for a while: their rudimentary shelter was inhabited, and despite its illegal status the authorities would have found it nearly impossible to do anything about it.

Alberto, commuting in the company's Alfa Romeo from his job to his new Spartan quarters, continued building and eventually became the owner of a two-story house with three apartments— one for himself and his wife, the other two for their teenage sons. Alberto was thinking big, planning ahead for the time when both boys would have families of their own.

Where Alberto betrayed real genius was the way he got water, sewers, electric power, and eventually a telephone connection for his far-out home. In innumerable visits to various city and state agencies—all on company time—and in follow-up telephone calls from his job, he eventually got all he wanted. Only someone who has had to cope with the daunting Roman bureaucracy can fully appreciate Alberto's achievements.

He probably tired local officialdom by his insistence, so that city agencies eventually gave in and connected his illegal out-of-the-way home with the utilities. It undoubtedly helped that Alberto had talked other people into buying plots near his home at still relatively low "farmland" prices, and advised them on how to start buildings of their own. Alberto, who can't have had any formal education beyond elementary school in his Umbrian village, found a lawyer who set up a cooperative consisting of himself and his new neighbors, and had himself elected its chairman.

His employers at the Rome publishing firm must have been immensely patient, because as Alberto's cooperative began flourishing, more and more phone calls from its members and from city offices arrived at its headquarters. The driver-messenger, whenever he wasn't on an errand for the company or his own operations, seemed always to be on the phone, taking care of his cooperative's business. True, a sizable portion of the telephone bills that Roman offices and firms get is generated by the private calls of their employees.

Over the years Alberto dealt with Roman bureaucrats as the spokesman first for dozens and eventually a couple of hundred home owners. They all were formally still outside the law, but they and their adult relatives were also voters. Alberto managed to line up political support from a major faction of the Christian Democratic Party, which was then influential in City Hall.

The driver-messenger's crowning feat as a real estate developer came when the city built an access road from the Via Cassia to his illegal hamlet where there had been only a dirt track earlier, which must have been hard on the suspension of Alberto's company Alfa Romeo. What's more, the city's transit authority extended the route of one of its bus lines for the convenience of the still nameless hamlet's inhabitants.

It seems that Alberto achieved this triumph by promising the office of the pope's cardinal-vicar for Rome that his cooperative would build its own church. It was about that time that I was once more riding in Alberto's company Alfa Romeo and listening, full of admiration, to his reports on the new highway link and bus route and on the proposed house of worship. "You'll get the pope himself to consecrate your church," I suggested jokingly. "I have been thinking of inviting His Holiness," Alberto said seriously.

Shortly afterward his cooperative struck the *condono* deal with the authorities, which made it legally respectable. Alberto collected his severance pay from the publishing firm and went into retirement to devote himself exclusively to his real estate ventures. I am sure he will charge the cooperative for every single phone call. The last I heard of him before today was that he had sued his long-indulgent former employers for a hefty amount of back pay that he claimed was due him for overtime he had worked without compensation.

The publishing firm, unable or unwilling to prove that the former driver-messenger had taken care of his private affairs during office hours and had made countless personal calls from office phones, settled out of court. Now the Christian Democratic Party's dominance in Rome's City Hall is a thing of the past, and I am sure Alberto's cooperative is no longer so keen on building a church. But Alberto doesn't have to fear the municipal bulldozers.

October

• Mailwoman •

Today we remained once more without mail. "Enza's kids must be sick again," a woman in our building observed from her balcony. Signora Enza is our letter carrier.

Enza is in her mid-thirties, and owing to her friendliness and presumed troubles she is well liked in our neighborhood. She is reliable in a way, though in another she isn't. I am not aware of any mail sent to us having ever been lost at the Rome end; delayed for days or weeks, yes. Enza's appearances are unpredictable.

Only the other day the newspapers announced that the postal administration and the mail workers' union had reached agreement on service improvements: there would henceforth be two mail deliveries on weekdays and one on Sunday. I remember several such promises over the years; right now we are lucky if we get mail four times a week. Once we remained an entire week without it.

Even the elder statesman who lives on our winding, rising street has apparently resigned himself to Enza's irregular service. He repeatedly served as Italy's prime minister and also presided over the United Nations General Assembly in New York for one year. He and his wife, who works in charities, must receive loads of mail.

When Enza does show up, she is pitied for having to lug the big, heavy leather bag bulging with letters, postcards, electric and telephone bills, magazines, and junk mail that have accumulated on the day or days she didn't work. A little handcart would ease her job, but the postal administration doesn't provide such equipment, and, despite all our compassionate noises, the householders in our section haven't gotten around to raising money to help out.

Fortunately Enza picks up the heap of mail she has to distribute from the Belsito post office on a square 450 feet above where we live, and can walk downhill while gradually emptying her bag. On her appointed rounds our courier descends the road down which the soldiery of Marius marched two thousand years earlier to slaughter his political enemies. That's why our hill is called the Monte Mario.

Though not one of the celebrated Seven Hills, it is higher than any of the seven, it is indeed the highest elevation within the municipal boundaries. By its name it is linked with one of the earliest of the many massacres Rome has endured. Today the Monte Mario is peaceful enough, and its flanks still look green, although the growing city has long invaded its lower slopes and its flat top. Many of the old cypress and pine trees still survive, but a few of them are charred every summer when patches of underbrush are destroyed by mysterious fires.

For several years a middle-aged mailman, Signor Giuseppe, came every working day. You could count on him to reach our palazzina, a residential building with thirteen apartments, by eleven A.M., when he would hand a presorted bundle destined for us to Nicolina, then our super. Nicolina would take the mail to her cubbyhole to divide it up, as she claimed, before putting it into the appropriate boxes. She was always up to date on everybody's personal affairs. Eventually we let her go, not because of her nosiness but because the condominium board decided we would save money by giving her the legal severance pay and closing the entrance door permanently.

After that, Signor Giuseppe had to call a resident on the intercom to get the door opened, whereupon he himself would put our mail into the boxes arrayed in the entrance hall. He never made a mistake.

One December morning Signor Giuseppe collapsed on the sidewalk near our building and was dead when the ambulance arrived. Had his extra-heavy bag, stuffed to overflowing with Christmas mail, set off his fatal heart attack? A group of neighborhood people sent a wreath to his funeral, and we all contributed to a cash gift for his widow, whom nobody knew. Most of us gave a little more than the amount of the tip that the dead man would have received anyway a week or so later. In Rome you customarily reward letter carriers for their pains with a gratuity at Christmas and Easter, although of course they are government workers who are not supposed to be tipped like waiters and cabbies.

Our next experiences with the postal service weren't happy. Every two or three weeks some other letter carrier, usually a forlorn-looking young woman, made a few appearances between gaps of two or three mail-less days, soon to be replaced by another neophyte. Checks that we had been assured were in the mail—and probably were, for a change—never arrived. We were told that a batch of mail addressed to people in our neighborhood had been found in a sanitation department Dumpster far from where we live, but we never saw those lost letters.

Mail for residents of our street, Viale Platone, was delivered to hallways of buildings with the same street number on Via Plotino. The city commission that has to come up with appellations for newly built-up sections obviously hadn't thought of the danger of mixups when it dedicated two adjacent streets in the same ZIP code area, 00136, to two ancient philosophers with names that in their Italian forms sound similar. Or maybe a learned member of the municipal body had wanted to make a pedantic point: wasn't Plotinus, the founder of the Neoplatonic school, an intellectual heir to Plato? At any rate, if one walks or drives along our Viale Platone to its upper end one reaches Via Plotino. If you summon a cab by phone, you'd better give detailed directions to the dispatcher, who may not be a classical scholar.

We have also a Via Aristotele in our neighborhood, and I cross the Via Tommaso d'Aquino every time I want to buy a newspaper. Street names in Rome often come in encyclopedic clusters—philosophers at the approaches to the Monte Mario, national heroes, great world figures, Italian and foreign cities, scientists, rivers, famous battles, and artists. The Via Milano intersects with the Via Palermo, although the northern metropolis and the capital of Sicily are far apart; the Piazza Cuba adjoins the Piazza Lituania; and the Viale Lincoln is near the Viale Shakespeare.

Before moving to the panoramic apartment on the Viale Platone we lived for ten years in a more central section that is a Who's Who of ancient Roman literature—Via Ovidio, Via Properzio, Via Plinio, Via Tacito, and so forth. Our street was the Via Tibullo. The Augustan elegist after whom it is named, Tibullus, was one of the first writers to praise Rome rhetorically as the Eternal City, *urbs aeterna*. He was also one of those Latin literati who again and again expressed yearning for the quiet and bliss of rural life, but whenever they did retreat to their country estates they would hanker for the congested and rumorous metropolis and were soon back.

We changed from the company of Latin men of letters to that of ancient sages above all because I was captivated by the views from the apartment on Viale Platone: to the right, quite close, we see Michelangelo's dome of St. Peter's; straight ahead, a mile or so away, are Capitol Hill and the Colosseum with the much more distant Alban Hills as a backdrop; to the left we behold the cream-colored Church of Trinità dei Monti on top of the Spanish Stairs, and the Pincio gardens. What's poor postal service against such vistas!

I have no trouble with outgoing mail. Like many other residents, I have for decades been mailing letters from the Vatican post office; trucks with State of Vatican City license plates take the postal bags to the airport, where they are loaded on planes bound for foreign destinations. Unfortunately, we cannot receive mail through the Vatican; only persons living or working in the papal state can. For us other Romans, there is the fax as an alternative, and the keen and efficient young men and women of private courier services ride up and down our street on their motorcycles and motor scooters several times a day.

As for Signora Enza, she at least doesn't mix up Viale Platone with Via Plotino. We got her some time after the business consultant who works out of his home on the ground floor of our building went up to the Belsito post office to complain about the terrible service. According to the consultant, the harassed office manager sighed: "You can't imagine, with all the jobless people we have in Rome, how hard it is for me to find a replacement for poor Signor Giuseppe. I'll end up delivering your mail myself."

Since Enza does bring our mail sooner or later, we don't complain anymore. She has two children who seem to be going through all possible infantile diseases (especially on Monday or when it rains), and she never mentions their father. Enza surely has enough problems of her own. Maybe she also does some moonlighting and hasn't always enough energy left to carry the heavy mailbag. We will soon see whether we actually receive the two deliveries on weekdays and one on Sunday that we have just been officially promised.

• Our Birds •

OCTOBER 13

The starlings are back, a myriad of them in swarm after serried swarm. From my terrace, as every autumn, I watch the dark flocks in the Roman sky, high above the roofs and domes as they continually cluster into new, bizarre shapes just before sunset. The birds suddenly turn simultaneously to fly in a different direction, change into funnel-like formations, split into subpatches, then join again.

Two separate swarms fly across each other, reminding me of a complicated ballet figure, a gymnastic display, or the maneuvers that highly trained cavalry squadrons perform at horse shows. Why do the starlings never collide with one another?

Today I spent a lot of time observing the birds' evolutions; at one point, eight different swarms, forever shifting, were in the air. It was the premiere of a free spectacle that will be on every late afternoon till December.

When dusk fell, the starlings alighted on trees to chat awhile and then sleep. Early tomorrow morning they will be gone. They leave a carpet of guano on sidewalks and the street; cars parked at curbsides overnight will be spattered all over. Even in dry weather, people waiting at the bus stop under the trees keep their umbrellas open: stand or walk there unprotected and you will have to send your clothes to the cleaners; you may also need a shampoo. The city's sanitation workers must undertake an extra scrubbing job from time to time, because the gummy street surfaces cause cars and buses to skid and motor scooters to lose control, spilling their riders.

This, however, happens only at a few spots in the city, the same ones year after year. The migratory birds don't descend on just any tree in Rome but always seek out certain green spots. Why just those special trees? It's one of several puzzles of starling behavior.

A long, straight avenue with two different names, Viale delle Milizie and Via Andrea Doria, lined with plane trees, a five-minute walk from where I live, has been a starling dormitory ever since I knew the neighborhood. The feathered migrants stay away from the plane trees on our street (I am not complaining!) and, for that matter, from the forested little hill in the Vatican Gardens nearby. Although my encyclopedia says starlings are omnivorous, they don't mingle with the fat, placid pigeons that thrive on generous handouts from tourists in St. Peter's Square.

We in our neighborhood strew birdseed on balconies, terraces, and windowsills for the sparrows, jays, and occasional blackbird or redbreast that visit us, but I have never spotted a starling among our guests. In addition Rome, like other European cities, has lately attracted certain birds, such as small falcons, that used to live only in the countryside and the mountains; they evidently have found that pickings are better where a lot of people live.

As for the starlings, ornithologists say they come in the fall from places in the north for a long rest stop in central Italy, and are particularly drawn to the green Sabine hills, roughly fifty miles east of Rome. There the birds devour insects, showing a particular liking for a kind of fly that infests olive trees with its larvae; thus the guests do useful pest control seven days a week, rain or shine. In the afternoon they quickly head to Rome to take refuge from owls and other nocturnal raptors. It seems the starlings also appreciate the relative warmth radiating from house walls, street lamps, and passing or parked cars during the cool nights. At dawn they head back to the Sabine region in large swarms.

The experts estimate that 800,000 to a million starlings spend their nights in this city in autumn; most of them seem to be from northern countries, but quite a few are indigenous, possibly hatched in or near Rome.

In their late afternoon frolics the starlings range all over Rome, but they alight only on the plane trees near where I live and on the evergreens along the street between the Central Railroad Terminal and the Piazza della Repubblica and in a nearby park, miles across the old town from our neighborhood.

Does each swarm always settle for the night in the same spot? Have some of the birds been here last year? Are instructions as to which areas to favor and which to shun encoded in their genes? Is there a chief bird in each flock that gives orders like a drill sergeant as to when to turn in flight and when to descend on the trees?

Residents in our part of Rome will doubtless petition City Hall, as every fall, to do something about what they call the "starling plague." The city has tried to scare away the unwanted guests by playing a taped rendering of their own distress call from truck-mounted loudspeakers. The starlings fled indeed but were soon back.

Some neighborhood people want the park department to cut down the planes, which suffer from various tree diseases anyway, but environmentalists oppose the radical proposal, contending that the trees aren't all that sick and may survive for decades to come if Rome's smog is curbed. Besides, if the birds were evicted from their current night quarters they would have to look for some other starling hostel, and there would be new complaints.

The present city administration, which is animal-friendly, is also mulling over a suggestion to replace the taped distress call with the starlings' mating call in an attempt to lure the bird flocks into the Villa Borghese gardens or another major park where they wouldn't bother anyone.

Regardless of these many attempts, our plane trees will have lost their last leaves before Christmas, and the starlings will be off because they don't like naked branches and twigs. They will drift off to the olive groves of southern Italy and await Spring to return to the north of the Continent.

• Baby Pensioners •

OCTOBER 14

This Friday lacks any distinctive mark in the calendar and is seemingly a working day like any other, but Rome this morning looked as if on vacation. Banks and public offices were closed, many stores were shuttered, and bands of teenagers who didn't have to go to school were joyously roaming the streets. Most of the espresso bars, however, were doing business, perhaps better than usual. When I had a morning cappuccino, I overheard the counterman and a patron boisterously gloating over the poor showing of the Milan soccer team in the new season's championship games. The general mood was relaxed. Our country's capital was participating in a nationwide general strike.

And yet this city with its many thousands of bureaucrats, its other white-collar workers, and its army of pensioners is vitally affected by what's at stake: the principal labor unions called the strike to protest a government plan to curtail retirement benefits. Staggering under a debt load of many trillions of lire, the treasury wants to increase the nation's productivity by making sure wage earners work until the age of sixty-five if they are men, or sixty-two if they are women.

I know a schoolteacher who quit her job at the age of forty-five; she is drawing her pension and now helps her daughter, who works in an office, to bring up two children. A friend of mine who toiled in a small machine shop went into retirement, with a sizable pension, when he was fifty. He now takes care of the bookkeeping in his wife's home-based fashion business and delivers coats and dresses to customers.

Thousands of other people in Rome (and many more elsewhere in the country) are enjoying what is known as "baby pensions." They managed to retire from government jobs at forty or thereabouts, some even at thirty-five, receiving for the rest of their lives substantial percentages of their last salaries.

At present two out of every five Italians get a pension, and in Rome the proportion is even more impressive. Some of the retirees I know have developed new second careers, like my friend who has become a pillar of his wife's second-floor fashion shop. Other pensioners just take it easy, read every line of *Il Messaggero* and *Corriere dello Sport* in the morning, saunter to the espresso bar at the corner around eleven A.M., indulge in two-hour naps after lunch, and watch television in the evening; still others talk about moving permanently to their native village in the Abruzzo or Umbria regions. Some actually do.

The labor leaders must know, as does any informed Italian, that the nation simply cannot afford the largesse of its retirement benefits. Yet the cuts that the government proposes, which in some form or other will have to be sanctioned by Parliament, are bound to hit millions of families, a good part of them in Rome. The prospect of having to work in one's job for much longer than expected causes much discontent. It's an issue involving masses of people that the unions cannot ignore, especially since they lost some of their former clout during the last couple of decades, owing to new conservative trends in Italian politics. The labor movement's chiefs must have decided that this new government move called for an immediate show of strength.

In the past, Italy's frequent strikes in a climate of social belligerency, were often scheduled for a Friday or Monday and were usually successful, regardless of whether workers wanted to obey union orders or just to enjoy a long weekend. Today's general strike was to be day-long for government personnel but to last only four hours in the morning for other workers. In Rome most people who took part in the stoppage did so during the entire day. The weather was fine for a trip to the countryside, as it often is this time of the year. Two families on our street piled children and picnic hampers into their cars and drove off early.

The subway and the buses didn't run today, but our electricity and telephone service remained unaffected. Out of curiosity and because of the nice weather I took a one-hour stroll across the city center to the Piazza della Repubblica, where a strike meeting was to be held.

The unions and left-wing political movements often pick that semicircular square near the Central Railroad Terminal for rallies that are expected to attract thousands of people; for larger demonstrations, when the organizers count on tens of thousands, the vast space in front of the Lateran Basilica is the usual venue.

In the Piazza della Repubblica the city of the ancient emperors, Renaissance popes, and turn-of-the-century architecture blends into an amalgam that is very Roman. When I first saw the square it was called Piazza dell' Esedra after the *exedra*, a giant western hall of the immense Baths of Diocletian. Extensive ruins of the thermae that Emperor Diocletian and his coemperors erected around A.D. 300—the largest public bathing establishment ever built in Rome—can still be seen on the northeastern side of the Piazza della Repubblica. The sumptuous vestibules, atriums, pools, steam chambers, dressing rooms, courts, and other spaces of Diocletian's thermae must have been able to accommodate simultaneously as many people as were to attend today's strike meeting, or even more.

Michelangelo, at the behest of Pope Pius IV, built in 1563–66 the Church of Santa Maria degli Angeli (St. Mary of the Angels) into what had been the *tepidarium*, a roofed hall with a lukewarm pool, of the ancient baths. The vast church is now being used for state funerals.

I remember the old Piazza dell' Esedra as a glamorous place, especially at night when a band of female instrumentalists would play popular music on a dais in front of many rows of café tables on the left one of two curved and arcaded buildings; those late-nineteenth-century structures rise where the apse of the *exedra* once stood. The café tables and chairs extended far into the piazza; beyond, ranks of off-duty uniformed soldiers and throngs of others stood for hours to listen to the music and applaud the violently rouged players and singers, presumably envying the smart patrons at the tables. Floodlights illuminated the large Fountain of the Naiads, four modern bronze groups of mermaids and sea monsters that had been put up in the center of the square in 1900.

The piazza was renamed in honor of the Italian Republic after a nationwide plebiscite voted out the Savoy monarchy in 1946. Seediness set in. The Piazza della Repubblica has become a traffic circus that pedestrians cross at their own risk—don't count on drivers to slow or stop just for you! Stairs at various points lead down to a subway station deep below. Recent immigrants, drifters, homeless people, drug peddlers, junkies, pickpockets, and muggers often spill into the square from the high-crime area around the railroad terminal.

Up until recently the Piazza della Repubblica and its approaches had to serve as a makeshift outdoor bus terminal. Thousands of passengers to and from Sicily, Naples, Umbria, Tuscany, and other parts of the country found little comfort there—no information booth, no marquees to protect them from rain, no toilets. You had to buy tickets from the driver of your coach, if you could find it. Last year City Hall ordered the long-distance coach operators to use instead an open space near the Tiburtina rail and subway stations (also devoid of amenities). Tourist buses nevertheless keep parking in or near the Piazza della Repubblica, perpetuating its ragged look.

After dark, weather permitting, a dispirited band still plays outside the café on the left side of the former *exedra,* but the audience isn't what it used to be; no savvy Roman would dream of spending an evening there. Adjacent to the musical café is an outlet of McDonald's whose restrooms, kept reasonably clean, are an asset to the entire neighborhood. At the other side of the café is an old cinema that now screens hard-core films. The whole area isn't outright grim, but it isn't welcoming either, especially at night, and it is an embarrassment to the august Grand Hotel, which looks out at the Piazza della Repubblica from its northeastern side.

This morning some five thousand people converged on the square for the strike rally. Most of them arrived from out of town in coaches chartered by the unions, which parked nearby; others came on foot in little groups, carrying streamers with antigovernment slogans, drumming on pasta pots they had brought from home and blowing whistles. Union leaders addressed the crowd, denouncing the ruling center-right coalition for its alleged designs to have the working class bear the brunt of the state's debt crisis. There were boos for the prime minister and the Manufacturers' Association, and cheers for the labor movement, but the mood appeared good-natured.

After an hour of oratory, thousands marched down the Via Nazionale, the thoroughfare that starts between the two curved buildings on the Piazza della Repubblica and leads downtown. Dark-painted vans of the Carabinieri and the state police preceded and escorted the noisy parade, but no incidents occurred. Quite a few of the marchers broke ranks to seek out espresso bars that had remained open, ignoring the general-strike call and serving a midmorning cappuccino to tired union militants.

• Famous Ancient Café •

OCTOBER 23

Policemen of the riot squad wearing crash helmets and wielding rubber truncheons were tearing into a crowd of screaming teenagers in the Via de' Condotti this afternoon just when I was on my way to meet a friend at the Antico Caffè Greco. I dodged into a side street, and it took some time before I could reach the venerable coffeehouse and sit down at one of its small round tables. My friend, who was waiting for me, told me the street clashes hadn't been caused by politics, as I thought, but by a fashion model, Claudia Schiffer.

Valentino, the renowned designer (his passport identifies him as Valentino Garavani), and his associate and companion Giancarlo Giammetti had contracted Ms. Schiffer to publicize their Rome-based firm. During several morning hours the blond German model, clad in Valentino creations, had been posing for a top photographer in various locations in the city center to produce stills reenacting scenes of the Fellini film La Dolce Vita.

Claudia Schiffer wasn't yet born when Fellini shot the 1959 picture that for the world at large would project an enduring image of presumed Roman sophistication. Actually, the movie was less true to Roman reality of the 1950s than, for instance, Thackeray's Vanity Fair is an authentic portrayal of early nineteenth-century London. No matter. Millions all over the world remain convinced that the languid hedonism of the beautiful, cynical people in the Via Veneto of La Dolce Vita is the real thing. Fellini once told me in an interview: "In my picture I invented a Via Veneto that never existed."

To stick to the indestructible clichés of La Dolce Vita, Ms. Schiffer had to prance in the Via Veneto and wade into the Trevi Fountain. When her handlers at last relented, she had a late spaghetti lunch at the palatial Valentino offices on the Piazza Mignanelli, off the Spanish Square. The fashion house keeps its headquarters in Rome, although Valentino has for several years staged his periodic shows in Paris, and his clothes are mostly sold abroad.

Throngs gathered around Ms. Schiffer and her troupe during each morning shoot. Local paparazzi (a term coined by Fellini) jostled to get their own piece of the action. When the supermodel at last could get her late takeout lunch, several hundred people were in the piazza below, yelling "Claudia, Claudia!" She showed herself on the balcony, prettily waved, and called down "Ciao!" Enthusiasm.

Things turned uglier when someone had the idea of letting Claudia pay a visit to the Bulgari jewelry shop, which happens to be next door to a Valentino boutique in the Via de' Condotti. Thousands quickly massed in the narrow, elegant shopping street, and there were fears that plate-glass windows might be shattered and high-priced merchandise vanish. It was then that the riot squad roared to the scene, and I thought an insurrection was being quelled. The police pushed the mob down the street, permitting Ms. Schiffer to get away safely.

Scores of passersby who, like me, had been caught in the scuffles in the Via de' Condotti had taken refuge in the Antico Caffè Greco and were crowding, three deep, in front of the espresso counter. Our elderly waiter, dignified in the frock coat that has remained a characteristic of the 230-year-old coffeehouse, sniffed: "It's a good thing they didn't bring *la tedesca* [the German woman] in here. We aren't that kind of place."

The guest book of the Antico Caffè Greco contains in its yellowed pages such names as Stendhal, Gogol, Baudelaire, Richard Wagner, D'Annunzio, Liszt, and Toscanini. Nikolai Gogol wrote much of his *Dead Souls* at the dark marble tabletops. The photos of famous visitors on the walls include one of Buffalo Bill, who with his Wild West exhibition was in Rome in 1903. I myself remember having often seen the aged painter Giorgio de Chirico holding court in the coffeehouse, always at the same corner table in the late morning. Today the long-landmarked Antico Caffè Greco offers one of the very few civilized indoor environments in the heart of Rome where one can sit down for quiet conversation.

The friend I was meeting is a member of a group of *romanisti,* professional and amateur scholars specializing in the city's history, architecture, art, and civilization, who hold informal gatherings once a month in the last of the six little rooms of the Antico Caffè Greco. He had something to say about today's fuss over the German fashion model. "Claudia Schiffer is a beautiful woman," he observed, "but it's sad that young Romans go crazy about her. It shows how provincial we have become, how we are starved for big-time glamour, how we are envious of Paris, of New York, of Hollywood, how we are being manipulated by television and the gossip magazines."

POSTSCRIPT, OCTOBER 27

Anita Ekberg, the former Swedish star who appeared in the episodes of Fellini's 1959 film that Claudia Schiffer replayed for Valentino earlier this week, also had a comment. In Buenos Aires, where she was visiting, she told an Italian interviewer: "Claudia Schiffer is nothing but a doll. She isn't an actress. *La Dolce Vita*, that's me."

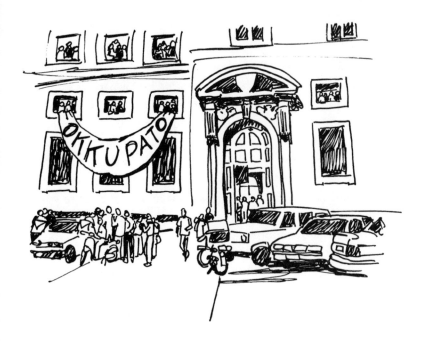

November

• Monster Exams •

Silvia, a pretty, dark-haired university graduate from Lecce in the heel of the Italian boot, is in Rome for only the third time in her life. Years ago, when she was still in high school, she was sightseeing here with her parents, whom we had earlier met and befriended during a vacation; more recently she had visited here with her fiancé. Silvia, who has been to Athens and Paris, told us yesterday she didn't really care for Italy's capital but had to come this time for an important reason: a job contest. It seems to be a lottery with discouraging odds, but Silvia has been looking unsuccessfully for work for the last two years, and she told us that her boyfriend in Lecce is also being supported by his parents.

Calling us from the railroad terminal upon her arrival yesterday, Silvia informed us she was included in the selection of ninety-three administrative assistants for the government's Ministry of the Cultural Patrimony; most of the winners in the competition would be assigned to museums and other institutions around the nation. The trouble is, 38,000 young women and men are vying for the jobs, which will pay something like the equivalent of one thousand dollars a month.

We offered to put up Silvia for the two nights she expected to stay in Rome, but she said she had been advised to make a reservation at the Ergife Palace Hotel, where the tests were to be held beginning this morning—in fact, she had sent an advance payment for a single room. The Ergife is an 804-room convention hotel on the Via Aurelia, on the city's western outskirts, looking out on the old highway to Pisa and Genoa.

The government occasionally rents the spacious meeting halls in the mammoth complex for mass examinations. Later yesterday we got another call from Silvia: when she had arrived at the Ergife, there was no single room for her despite her reservation. The reception desk had been beleaguered by other young people, and the harried clerk had eventually told her that all he could do for her was to put her in a room with three other women; they would have to sleep in a double bed and two makeshift bunks. Silvia said okay, though she had never seen her prospective roommates (who were also strangers to one another); she wanted to know whether she could still stay with us if she felt uneasy with the other three. We said Yes, of course, but we didn't hear from Silvia again last night.

It turned out to be a good idea for her to stay at the hotel behemoth. This morning it would have been hard for her to reach it in time for the tests. True, the Ergife had sent a hotel bus to pick up candidates for the examination at the Via Ottaviano subway stop not too far from where we live, but who knew about it? The municipal transit system had beefed up its Nos. 246 and 994 bus routes with additional runs to the Via Aurelia, but traffic on the initial stretch of the highway was stalled for miles in the early morning, and the extra police officers dispatched to the area had difficulty unsnarling it. A similar congestion occurred in the Flaminio section in the city's north, where the overflow of candidates, eight thousand of them, were to take the exam in the Palazzetto dello Sport, a hall where basketball games and other athletic events are normally held.

Today's job competition was by no means the biggest to take place in Rome lately. Last month no fewer than 74,000 young men flocked to the capital, seeking to qualify for one of a few hundred openings in the ranks of the Finance Guard, Italy's fiscal police.

Rome, citadel of bureaucracy since the times of the ancient emperors, periodically sees such invasions by young job seekers from all corners of the country, especially from the deep south, where opportunities for work in the private economy are scarce. The candidates have to pay their own expenses for a chance in the sweepstakes for government employment. To house, feed, and screen them is a local industry, like taking care of religious pilgrims and tourists.

This afternoon Silvia reported to us by phone: "The three other girls in my room and I got along well enough, although we are of course rivals; two are also from the south and the other one is from near Florence. This morning after a cafeteria breakfast we were seated at individual small desks in an enormous concrete hall and had to fill in questionnaires and write essays as if we were again taking high school graduation exams. Tomorrow the tests will continue and end. How did I do? I don't know. Those of us who are eventually chosen will be notified in weeks, maybe months. But some of us here at least have found new friends."

• Disco Delights •

NOVEMBER 6

When I went to meet a young French Embassy attaché and his wife at their new place in the Trastevere section last night, I had no idea we would end up in a discotheque. I am not crazy about nightclubs in general and have always sought to stay away from those in Rome. The diplomat has recently been assigned to the Italian capital and, having settled in, asked me for drinks at his apartment; he or his wife got my phone number from a friend in Paris.

It's fashionable now to live in Trastevere, the once-plebeian district between the right Tiber embankment and the slope of the Janiculum, which for some years has been overrun by moneyed Italian sophisticates and by foreigners. "This is the Montparnasse of Rome," the diplomat's wife, a svelte Parisienne, twittered. Trastevere indeed has become arty and cosmopolitan; rents of course have skyrocketed; basements and lofts in medieval houses have been converted into the studios of painters, sculptors, and graphic designers.

The small fifth-floor apartment that the French couple found through a real estate agent is in a cramped old house on a narrow, noisy street; no elevator. The staircase must have been white-washed only recently. My hosts let me have a look at the kitchen and bathroom, which the landlord had modernized, and told me about the red tape involved in shipping their furniture from Paris to Rome. Then they proudly led me out onto their terrace. I voiced the admiration that was expected, and meant it. The panorama, unimpaired by last evening's drizzle, embraced the twinkling lights on the long ridge of the Janiculum on one side, and the floodlit Capitol Hill and the white marble heap of the Victor Emmanuel Monument on the other. "That view is worth climbing up those stairs," the diplomat said.

Another couple, Italians, had meanwhile arrived, and our hosts suggested after a glass or two of champagne we all adjourn to a nearby pizzeria, "the trendy thing to do," as madame observed with a dash of self-irony. The pizzeria had an oven with a wood fire conspicuously in sight—no microwave treatment of frozen pizza here!—and attractive table linen. The menu listed a dozen kinds of pizza, including a "carpaccio" variety, new to me, that turned out to be simply slices of fresh mozzarella and other soft cheeses covering the basic product, which was gratifyingly thin and crisp.

The red wine that we ordered, alas, was icy, clearly just pulled out of the refrigerator. The Frenchman, in workable Italian, lectured the young waiter on red wines requiring room temperature, which apparently struck the fellow as an extravagance of foreigners; he promised to report the complaint to the manager, who he said would come later. We chatted awhile about Italian and French politics, and eventually the attaché's wife, a little bored, proposed: "Let's go to a disco."

The Italian husband and wife said that most of Rome's discotheques were crowded with teenagers but that Gilda, near the Spanish Square, was in a different class, this season's hot ticket. All five of us squeezed into a taxi, which had been summoned by phone, and drove across the Tiber into the city center. During the short trip I told my companions I knew quite a number of middle-aged Roman women—now that I think about it again, actually only three—called Gilda. The name was felt to be glamourous in the nineteen-fifties because of a film starring Rita Hayworth as "Gilda" (the way

Pamela was fashionable in the nineteen-eighties). Ms. Hayworth was at the height of her beauty and fame when I saw her during a press reception, in a place on the Monte Mario on Rome's northern outskirts, to publicize her latest picture. The photographers, then not yet called paparazzi, couldn't seem to get enough shots of her, and the star, who was to die of Alzheimer's disease more than thirty years later, was laughing and seemed happy.

The Gilda piano bar, late-hours restaurant, and discotheque in the Via Mario de' Fiori is the elegant showcase of the entrepreneur Giancarlo Bornigia, whom the gossip writers often call the king of Roman nightlife. He knows how to get publicity.

When we arrived at Gilda, the place was filling up to celebrate, as we were told, the birthday of a local soft-porn starlet known as Milly d'Abbraccio (*abbraccio* is Italian for embrace). The Italian woman in our party said she occasionally saw the scandal magazines at her hairdresser's, and had read that Milly had recently changed from a redhead into a blonde, and a month ago had had a baby boy, her second child. (Nobody ever admits to buying *Eva Express* and similar publications; one just happened to have distractedly leafed through them at the hairdresser's or in the dentist's waiting room.)

Despite her new motherhood, for a few minutes Milly stripped to the waist; most patrons applauded the proud display, while the Italian at our table muttered, "Gilda didn't use to be that kind of place." Paparazzi who had been waiting in the wings, probably alerted by Gilda's press agent, snapped picture after picture.

I stayed on a little, while madame was dancing with the slightly scandalized Italian, and his wife with the attaché, but I soon excused myself. As I was leaving, around midnight, new guests were still arriving; I thought I recognized faces I must have seen on television, but couldn't place them.

• It's Getting Chilly •

I should have preferred to be grilled in a four-hour income-tax audit rather than be forced to sit through last night's meeting of our condominium board, but there was no way out. We are facing an emergency and had to decide what to do. Rust has gnawed through the building's boiler, and indoors it's getting quite chilly, especially at night, although Rome's weather is still mild.

We learned that not only was the boiler busted and unable to deliver any heat, but it threatened to flood the basement of our building. The official heating period in Rome starts on November 15, but the consultant who lives and works on the ground floor insisted we ignore the law and get warmth right away. The consultant's home receives much less sunshine than ours, and he used to complain about poor heating even when the boiler worked at full steam—imagine now!

The thirteen apartment owners of our condominium never agree on anything that concerns us all, and board meetings are always lengthy and tedious before a majority decision is reached. Luckily, the boiler problem isn't one of those that legally require unanimity, like the much-needed repair of the building facades, which will be tackled only when the city's housing department at last orders us to do it after patches of mortar or an entire balcony have crashed to the ground (let's hope nobody gets hurt!).

Emergencies like the present one are common in Rome, where most people live in condominium apartments. After the heat is turned off—by law, not before March 15—in our buildings, nobody looks after the boilers and pipes. Defects and breakdowns are discovered only after the first cold snap in the fall, when residents clamor for warmth in their homes, and a scramble for spare parts, plumbers, and mechanics sets in.

I am sure the ancient Romans, who had splendid engineers, provided timely and better maintenance for their public and private baths and for their palaces and villas. The dwellings of the poor might collapse or be gutted by flames, as the contemporary satirists complain, but the luxurious homes of the rich were cozy in the Roman winter, thanks to hot-water conduits under the floors and in the walls. Slaves kept the fires and boilers going and the indoor temperatures toasty.

The heating systems and the kitchen ranges almost everywhere in our city now depend on methane that comes from the gas fields in Algeria through underwater pipelines across the Mediterranean. From time to time we hear of vague threats by Arab nationalists that they might cut gas supplies to Europe, but the feeling here is that whoever is in power in Algeria needs the revenues from the gas sales overseas. Should the pipelines be sabotaged, there are always the substantial supplies of natural gas that northern Italy receives from Siberia, Norway, and the Netherlands, some of which might be diverted to the nation's capital.

When I moved to Rome in 1938 most people in the city roughed winters in their apartments and workplaces without any heating at all or with only rudimentary sources of warmth. On a chilly April day of that year I visited Senator Francesco Salata, whom I knew because he had been Italian ambassador in Vienna. He received me with his overcoat on; the ornate room of the Palazzo Madama, the seat of the upper house of Parliament, where we met, was icy as was the entire building.

During the next few years my young wife and I weathered the cold months at home thanks to the layers of woolens that we were wearing, and with a *scaldino,* a little iron stove in which charcoal was kept glowing with the help of a hand-held fan. A great many

Roman families lived likewise through the winter. For several years I was recurrently astonished that sunny Italy could be so cold.

From November to spring many local men, including high officials, wear pullovers or cardigans under their suit jackets; women, too, resort to plenty of wool. Homes, offices, restaurants, and cafés here are still underheated or outright drafty.

Getting heat in our apartments during the quickly approaching chilly period was the principal item on the agenda of our condominium meeting last night. It was held in the office of our *amministratore* in the upscale Parioli section on the other side of the Tiber. A certified accountant, he manages our building and scores of others with the aid of two female employees and a computer.

Years ago our condominium dismissed our *portiera*, chatty Nicolina, who combined the functions of doorman and live-in superintendent; since then, whenever the elevator breaks down (about once a week) or something else has to be repaired, someone must call the office of the *amministratore*. It is usually days before action is taken and someone shows up to fix the elevator or put in a new lightbulb on one of the landings. The building entrances (we have two of them on different levels) are now permanently locked. If you have no key you must ask a resident by intercom to open the door electronically.

Why did the board fire Nicolina? A majority of apartment owners said the condominium would save money by doing so: it wasn't so much her small salary that was considered but the social security contributions for her that we had to pay. I was for retaining Nicolina but was overruled. She collected a sizable sum as severance pay, which helped her buy an apartment of her own in a distant part of the city. The two rooms and tiny kitchen in our building where she and her pampered boy had been living became a rent-paying office of an outfit that manufactures neon publicity signs in a nearby garage. That enterprise, however, owes us several months' rent, another item to be discussed last night. We discussed and quarreled for four hours. At the end I felt a headache coming on.

• A Million in the Streets •

NOVEMBER 12

Today the city saw the largest demonstration anyone can remember—much larger even than the "oceanic" rallies that heard Mussolini's harangues from his balcony. The principal labor unions, which organized the impressive antigovernment protest, claim that 1.5 million people from all over Italy took part in it; the police estimate there were 750,000 to 800,000.

From early morning to the afternoon Rome traffic was at a near standstill as the masses marched in the streets, gathered in three different squares to listen to inflammatory rhetoric, and then swarmed good-naturedly around the city. The subway kept functioning but was packed like Tokyo commuter trains at rush hour.

Walking across the center I saw groups of demonstrators waving red banners, carrying portraits of Lenin and Che Guevara and shouting obscenities aimed at the prime minister (who spent the day at home, near Milan). There was, however, no violence to speak of except for a scuffle between police and a band of ultraleftists gathering in the vast Piazza di San Giovanni. The police reported that twenty-five of their own men suffered injuries; no word about civilian casualties.

The other two rallies were held in the Piazza del Popolo and near the Circus Maximus. Strolling along the Tiber embankment, I reached the ancient circus with the sparse remains of the biggest racecourse of the imperial age, and wondered how many spectators could have watched the chariot contests in it then—a hundred thousand, twice that number? Today the crowd filled the entire vast space around the oblong excavation site and a part of the street leading to the Colosseum.

A man standing near me received a call on his cellular phone and responded in a southern dialect. I gathered he was communicating with his wife or girlfriend who had come with him to Rome and who had gone shopping instead of taking in the political oratory; it seemed she had found quite a few stores open. During the following hours I heard the ringing of *telefonini* (cellular phones) again and again: this was a high-tech crowd.

The weather was glorious; after several rainy days the sky was cloudless and the sun warm. When the speech making and slogan shouting were over, the demonstrators besieged refreshment stands that had sprouted all around and lined up at portable toilets that the city had thoughtfully readied for the occasion. Rome's mayor, a leader of the Green movement who had been elected with left-wing support, was on the Circus Maximus grandstand.

Many of the provincials who had come to Rome for the protest used the sunny afternoon for sightseeing, picnicking, and picture taking. When I passed the Colosseum on my long march home, the giant travertine hulk was teeming with people, but the young Eritrean who sells little plastic models of the monument and other cheap souvenirs complained, "Nobody buys nothing."

Today's invasion of the city, peaceful though it was, had been planned as a warning to the government and Parliament not to follow through on proposals to cut entitlements and social services. The four-hour nationwide general strike and the rally in the Piazza della Repubblica on October 14 appeared in hindsight to have been only a first rumble of what may become a political earthquake.

Organized labor has seemed on the decline during the last several years, but the austerity program of the ruling center-right coalition has handed a welcome issue to the unions. Today's giant demonstration proved that they are again riding high on a wave of popular discontent; millions of wage earners and retirees are afraid above all that Italy's generous pension system will be whittled down.

The left-wing parties, including diehard Communists, clearly view the present unrest as a chance for a comeback after their defeat in last March's general elections. Prominent leftists attended today's rallies, but the organizing and speech making were all done by labor officials.

Today's performance belied the stereotype of Italians as terrible organizers, brilliant though they may be when improvising. Prussian general staff officers couldn't have mapped the mobilization of a million demonstrators better. The state railways, prodded by the unions, brought tens of thousands to Rome and transported them home again in fifty special trains. Others made the trip in one of eight thousand charter buses. Thousands of Sardinians sailed to the mainland and back in ferryboats making extra runs. And thousands of out-of-town cars were parked in the suburbs.

The most striking impressions of the city streets and squares flooded with masses of people were captured by helicopter-mounted television cameras. Tonight, however, a government supporter told a television interviewer that, yes, a million Italians may have demonstrated in the capital, but that among the fifty-four million who stayed at home there were many who were convinced that the nation must tighten its purse strings.

• Toward the Third Millennium •

NOVEMBER 14

Today the pope formally began to promote the Holy Year 2000, stressing that the second millennium of Jesus Christ's birth should be celebrated not only in Rome but also in the Holy Land and throughout the world. Romans, however, have started seriously considering the challenges and opportunities that the exceptional church event will bring. More than any other city, Rome expects to profit economically from the Holy Year, serving as host to twenty or thirty million pilgrims and tourists.

The Roman solemnities in 2000 will peak in an International Eucharistic Congress that will draw large crowds, though probably not the one million people who demonstrated against the Italian government here last Saturday.

This city has coped with friendly invasions of the faithful since the Middle Ages. Dante, for instance, mentions the multitudes he saw crossing the Tiber bridge in front of the Castel Sant'Angelo, then a papal fortress guarding access to the Vatican, during Christianity's first jubilee year in A.D. 1300.

As with past Holy Years, the forthcoming commemoration will again bless Rome with plenty of money—and an inevitable harvest of troubles. Municipal officials are already worried about how to assure a measure of mobility to tens of thousands of visitors—hundreds of thousands on some days—as well as to the residents themselves. During last Saturday's parades and rallies the city was virtually paralyzed for many hours; could it endure such crippling situations for weeks and months?

For more than a decade no strategic attempt has been made to ease Rome's growing traffic woes. In preparation for the Olympic Games in the summer of 1960, a new beltway, the Via Olimpica, was built, along with some street underpasses closer to the city's center. Since then these routes have always been heavily traveled. In the late 1970s, the subway's Line A was constructed; it is now a vital transit route, but the stop nearest the Vatican, Via Ottaviano, is two-fifths of a mile away from St. Peter's Square. By the year 2000 the subway system will be extended to outlying districts, yet pilgrims will still have to walk ten busy city blocks from the

Ottaviano station to St. Peter's. Plans for a new C Line from the Colosseum to the Vatican are still vague.

The bulky tourist coaches in which many, if not most, pilgrims will arrive in 2000 are already a major headache to traffic planners. There are no adequate parking spaces anywhere near the Vatican. Last Saturday the eight thousand buses that brought the demonstrators to town were parked on the outskirts, and from there five different parades surged along main streets to the squares where the rallies took place. The Vatican and the organizers of pilgrimages will instead insist that Holy Year coaches may take travelers—many of whom will inevitably be elderly, infirm, or both—to points as close to St. Peter's as possible. This will be interesting to see, as even the few dozen tourist buses currently ferrying people to the pope's general audiences on Wednesdays and back to their lodgings cause traffic jams in a large area around the Vatican. Yet, as usual, the Vatican will get what it wants.

Providing accommodations and meals for Holy Year pilgrims will be easy and gainful tasks; the Romans have gladly tackled them for centuries. In addition to the city's eight hundred hotels and pensions, totaling sixty thousand beds, a growing number of religious houses are taking in paying guests. As the number of novices in monasteries and convents declines, there is plenty of vacant space. Many ecclesiastical communities have converted parts of their premises or entire buildings into boardinghouses. There, guests live in clean rooms with modern facilities, get wholesome meals, and may even relax over a drink or two at a house bar. In some of these hospices a ten P.M. or eleven P.M. curfew is the rule; in others a guest who wants to have a night on the town gets a latchkey.

Alsatian friends of mine recently stayed at a hilltop guest house operated by an American-based order. It was a mere ten-minute stroll south of St. Peter's Square, and my friends raved about the cheerfulness and efficiency of the Franciscan sisters running the place and about its garden with tall pine trees. If they ever were to revisit Rome, they said, they certainly knew where to stay.

The Holy Year 2000 will undoubtedly induce various religious communities to ready new facilities for pilgrims. The Holy See itself has nearly completed a sixty-five-foot-tall building, five floors of which will house visiting bishops and other prelates, to replace an undistinguished old structure in the southeast corner of Vatican City. The construction project caused angry protests from local environmentalists during the previous two years on the grounds that the new edifice obstructs the only good view of the dome of St. Peter's from the south. The critics complained to the Italian Parliament, government, and head of state, and even to the United Nations Educational, Scientific, and Cultural Organization, but to no avail. The Holy See, which is a sovereign entity and on its tiny territory can—at least theoretically—do what it likes, ignored the protests.

Near St. Peter's Square, the owner of the stationery store whose customer I have been for years told me the other day that rents, especially for street-level space, are going up around the entire neighborhood. Entrepreneurs, it seems, are planning to open new espresso bars, gelato parlors, fast-food outlets, and souvenir shops. A Holy Year business boom around Vatican City has already started.

The pope didn't mention business in the Apostolic Letter that the Vatican issued today to the Roman Catholic hierarchy and the faithful world-wide. The seventy-page document will, as usual, be known and quoted by the opening words of its Latin text (translated from John Paul II's Polish original), *Tertio Millennio Adveniente* (As the third millennium is approaching). The letter was presented to the international press this morning by Cardinal Roger Etchegaray, the French-Basque prelate who directs preparatory work for the jubilee year. Quite a few Vatican insiders think

Etchegaray, formerly archbishop of Marseilles, may be the next pope. John Paul II must be aware of such speculation; perhaps the Frenchman is his own candidate for succession.

During the last several weeks, people inside and outside of the Vatican have been spreading rumors that the pope is critically ill. They must have been startled by a passage in today's Apostolic Letter that, in veiled form, seemed to express John Paul II's hope to be alive and well in the Holy Year, when he will be eighty years old. "It would be very significant," he wrote, "if on occasion of the year 2000 it were possible to visit all those places that are on the road of the People of God" from Abraham and Moses to the conversion of the Apostle Paul near Damascus. John Paul II has repeatedly said he wanted to make a pilgrimage to Mount Sinai and the Holy Land.

• The Okkupation •

NOVEMBER 19

"OKKUPATO" read the black letters on a bedsheet strung up under a red banner between two third-floor windows of the Ennio Quirino Visconti High School. Hundreds of students have taken over the front wing of the four-hundred-year-old building, a brick mastodon on the central Piazza del Collegio Romano that was once a Jesuit college. They pretend to keep the state institution going by "self-management," and some of them sleep in classrooms at night while others slink home after dark.

The Italian word for "occupied" of course is spelled with two c's, but the young squatters modified the spelling to make it look menacing. The letter *k* is a foreign intruder in the Italian alphabet; it is used only for extraneous words and phrases, and oddly enough is indicated by the German term *Kursaal* ("spa casino") in Italy's official spelling code. *K* is felt to be outlandish, barbarian (although classical Greek used it!), even slightly sinister. During the 1970s I have seen here plenty of demonstrators brandishing signs and carrying streamers denouncing the misdeeds of "Amerika." The implication was that the United States was a Nazi monster.

This time, the k's in OKKUPATO seem to proclaim, as do the red flags, that the Kommunists are back. The militant leftists of Visconti High and of more than eighty other public schools around Rome are in fact protesting the current center-right government and especially its fiscal and education policies. The contention is that there aren't enough funds for the public schools, while Italy's rulers are subsidizing private institutions and in general favoring the rich.

Some teachers support the student activists; others prudently stay at home and wait for the present unrest to blow over. In some schools the leaders of the "okkupation" have invited sympathetic journalists, writers, or media personalities to hold classes on such subjects as "History of the Italian Women's Movement" or "The Philosophy of Comic Strips." The kids attending those lectures won't earn any credits.

The Association of High School Principals deplored the agitation in a statement, warning that end-of-term exams will cover the entire scholastic programs regardless of whether teachers had a chance to go through them in their classes. The philosophy of comic strips won't be much help in solving geometry problems.

I have been told that a few members of the government suggested the police be ordered to go into the occupied schools and throw the rebellious students out. This would be easy enough if the prime minister and a majority in the cabinet hadn't opposed such drastic action.

Student protests are an annual rite in Rome, performed in November as unfailingly as the starlings descend on us in October. Only the ostensible motivations of the students change. Over the years I have heard marching youngsters shout "Hands off

Cuba!" "Get out of Vietnam!" and slogans voicing solidarity with Palestinians or Nicaraguans. The underlying reality is probably that the teenagers, after six weeks of class work, feel it's time for a little action. Any topical issue will do. School officials know from long experience that the demonstrations will eventually run out of steam and that many parents will get impatient and tell their offspring to curb their political passion and take up their textbooks for a change. High school girls in particular get an earful at home about their revolutionary ardor being suspect if it entails sleeping out, even if only in classrooms.

What's new this year is that student neofascist groups appear to have become stronger than ever since the fall of Mussolini. For decades they have been a small sect, ostracized and often beaten up by their left-wing classmates. Now the young rightists who curiously call themselves the Ancestors hold rallies of their own and seem even to be dominant in some schools; but they go along with the "okkupiers." So far there has been little student violence, and apparently a lot of delicious boy-girl fun.

Today a few thousand university and high school students paraded from the Colosseum (Kolosseum?) to the Chamber of Deputies, lustily yelling insults addressed at the government. Some of the marchers wore kaffiyehs; the black-and-white headdress of Palestinian men has long been a badge of male and female student radicals here. The weather was fine, and everybody, including the police, appeared to be having a good time.

• Clerical Fashions •

NOVEMBER 26

It wasn't hard to get admitted to this morning's ceremony in the Vatican for the installation of thirty new cardinals by Pope John

Paul II. Technically, the solemn rite was a public consistory; it turned out to be a clerical ballet before thousands of people in the huge, concrete audience hall near the southern flank of St. Peter's.

The new international princes of the church brought with them relatives, friends, fans, and parishioners; the groups that had come to Rome to witness the installation of the four Italians among the thirty neocardinals were particularly large.

Few Romans were apparently in today's crowd. The public in this city, traditionally blasé about the Vatican, was mostly unaware of this morning's event, the sixth time in the sixteen years of John Paul II's pontificate that he handed out red hats. Most people here distractedly learned of the consistory only from a brief sequence on tonight's television news. For Vatican City, however, and for the monasteries, convents, and religious hospices where the new cardinals and their followers are guests during their sojourn here, this is an exciting period.

The last few days were also a busy time for the city's ecclesiastical tailors and outfitters. Weeks ago the Vatican's Office of Liturgical Celebrations sent a sixteen-page brochure to all nominees to the cardinalate, detailing the dress code they must observe in Rome. For today's ceremony, for instance, they had to appear in a red cassock with a fringed red sash, red stockings, and black shoes; and to wear a pectoral cross on a red-and-gold silk string, a bishop's ring, a white lace surplice, and a red skull-cap. The cross and ring used to be gold, but nowadays any metal will do.

Some of the apparel that the correctly dressed prince of the church needs is also available abroad, above all in countries with strong Roman Catholic traditions; however, the specialized stores in Rome that cluster near the Pantheon and the Vatican are up to date on clerical fashions and possess unsurpassed know-how in their arcane field. Virtually all the new cardinals became their clients and had their last fittings during the days preceding this morning's ceremony.

At the culmination of the lengthy rite today, the pope presented each of the twenty-nine attending nominees with the scarlet biretta (a three-ridged, square priest's hat) that is the badge of their new dignity. The thirtieth neocardinal, the aged French theologian Yves Congar, will receive his biretta from the pope's nuncio in a Paris clinic.

As the new cardinals filed past the white-clad pope and many of the old members of the Sacred College were looking on, the vast audience applauded as at a gala show—a symphony in white, scarlet, red, and purple. There were loud cheers for the oldest among the honorees, Mikel Koliqi, the Roman Catholic primate of Albania who has spent forty-four of his ninety-two years in prison and detention camps. The archbishop of Sarajevo, Vinko Puljic, in his early forties and the youngest among today's recipients of the red hat, got the loudest applause, an emotional demonstration of sympathy for the tortured Bosnian capital.

In an address, John Paul II lamented that there was still no prospect of peace in Bosnia-Herzegovina where "so much innocent blood is being shed." His was comparatively bland pontifical oratory, careful not to take sides or assign blame in the face of the Balkan tribal war that has shown up the impotence of the United Nations, the European Union, international diplomacy, and the Vatican.

The pope spoke in Italian rather than Latin this morning in his role as bishop of Rome. Historically, the Sacred College developed from the medieval body of the city's parish priests; officially, each cardinal is the pastor of one of Rome's many churches. In the next few days each recipient of the red hat will take ceremonial possession of his "titular church" in the city that the bishop of Rome—John Paul II—has assigned to him.

The college of cardinals is sometimes called the Senate of the Church, but it has no legislative powers. The pope is an absolute monarch, the supreme lawgiver, judge, and ruler of Roman Catholicism. John Paul II and his predecessors have on some occasions summoned all cardinals to the Vatican for consultation, but they didn't have to do so, nor did they have to heed the recommendations of their "senate." The only real power that the Sacred College as a body wields is to run the Holy See after the death of a pontiff, and to choose a successor in secret conclave.

Quite a few of the prelates who were given the red hat today couldn't take part in a conclave even if it were to be held tomorrow, because they are overage. Pope Paul VI, in a rare gesture of pontifical ageism, decreed in 1970 that cardinals are barred from participation in a papal election after their eightieth birthday. They still belong to an exclusive international club, like the group of Nobel Prize winners, are addressed as "Your Eminence," and enjoy other privileges. There is even a very remote chance that an octogenarian cardinal, perhaps a saintly man, might one day become pope. Though he is beyond the age limit for casting a vote in the election of a new pontiff, a cardinal still remains eligible for the papacy.

• Derby Thrills •

NOVEMBER 27

Today was the Sunday of the Derby with all its traditional excitement, but in Rome the crowning sports event has nothing to do with horses. Pronounced DAIRR-bee, it is the championship match between the two local first-division soccer clubs, the Lazio and the Roma. This afternoon 83,000 people filled the Olympic Stadium to the last cranny. They witnessed the Roma beating its perpetual rivals three to nought in a game the team dominated from beginning to end, confounding the forecasters.

The fans of the winning team, the *romanisti,* were delirious while militant *laziali,* supporters of the losers, started wrecking the stadium's north curve, where they had been segregated, and fought with the police. As I am writing I still hear the noise of firecrackers and car horns rising from the lower-lying neighborhoods. The city-wide celebration of the Roma enthusiasts will go on until night.

Tomorrow, in espresso bars, trattorias, offices, and workshops all over Rome, grim *laziali* who had been betting on their team's triumph will have to pay off their debts to gloating *romanisti*—treating them to cappuccinos with pastries or to lunch, wearing the colors (yellow and purple) of the hated Roma for a day, or sweeping floors.

Soccer divides the city emotionally into two tribes much the way the chariot races in ancient Rome agitated the entire populace, pitting the Greens against the Reds. In present-day Rome you must be a professed fan of either the Roma or the Lazio even if you secretly don't care for soccer, otherwise you are considered an outsider or a detestable snob. There are probably more *romanisti* than *laziali.* I have always sympathized with the Lazio, which has long been the underdog and for a time was even demoted to second division, the also-rans of professional soccer. This season, however, the Lazio had so far been doing well, ranking above the Roma in the championship table.

Rome's mayor, Francesco Rutelli, lately avowed his support for the Lazio, which may cost him *romanista* votes in the next election. Today he looked increasingly dejected when the Roma scored the first and second goals, and he left the stadium's VIP enclosure before the end of the game. The mayor's wife, Barbara Palombelli, a successful journalist, watched the match on television; she is an all-out *romanista*. This is not an unusual situation; soccer allegiance here cuts through families and ideological camps.

According to rumor, the bishop of Rome—Pope John Paul II— is a closet *romanista*. Some of the Polish nuns who run his household in the Vatican are said to be rooting for the Lazio.

Both Roman clubs count left-wingers and right-wingers, political moderates and extremists, wealthy and poor people, university professors and bus drivers among their *tifosi*. A *tifoso* is someone affected by soccer fever of typhus (*tifo*) intensity, and if you aren't, you'd better pretend to be.

I have always heard that the social mix is particularly interesting in the Lazio camp, said to include Roman princes and proletarians, whereas the middle class tends to favor the Roma; but there are no statistics or polls to prove or disprove such stratification.

Italians who move to Rome from some other region may sentimentally watch the fortunes of their hometown clubs, the Palermo or the Juventus of Turin for instance, but they will soon be sucked into the local soccer scene and end up as adoptive *romanisti* or *laziali*. I know quite a few expatriates who are genuine supporters of one of the two Roman clubs, or make a show of being *tifosi* in order to blend with the natives. For an elected official here it would be political suicide to betray indifference toward soccer.

Among my friends and acquaintances in Rome are some who have shifted their political orientation—former Communists who declare to be liberal democrats today, and former fascists who have long cast their ballots for the Christian Democrats or the Communists. I know no Lazio fan who has become a *romanista* or the other way around.

In fact, if you ask a native male Roman to define himself in one word, the chances are he will say *laziale* or *romanista* rather than "Italian" or "physician" or "Catholic" or "optimist." Many thousands of

Roman women had long pitied themselves as soccer widows when their men hurried to the stadium after an early Sunday lunch, leaving them sulking at home. Television, almost entirely devoted to the national spectator sport on Sunday afternoons, has changed all that: women too have fallen prey to *tifo,* and are seen in rising numbers in the bleachers.

Today's Derby was surrounded by tighter security precautions than usual: three thousand Carabinieri soldiers and men and women of the state police guarded the stadium as well as all approaches to it, and strategic points throughout the city. A fleet of ten police and air force helicopters was in readiness, but not all of them left the ground. The reason for such special measures was what happened in Brescia, 330 miles to the north, last Sunday.

Three hundred *romanisti* of the rabid faction known as the "ultras" had chartered a railroad train and traveled to the northern city for the Roma versus Brescia championship match. The game resulted in a nought-to-nought draw while the "ultras" were rioting. The ensuing grave incidents were not quite unexpected, because there is a history of clashes between Roma and Brescia supporters. Last Sunday their old hostility flared up again even before the match started, and the police were drawn into the fights. Result: Brescia's deputy police chief was hospitalized with knife wounds and a broken nose, another police officer was injured by a firecracker, and some thirty *tifosi* of either side were hurt. A dozen "ultras" were arrested and tried next morning in extra-quick proceedings; all but one of them could return to Rome after plea-bargaining deals and suspended sentences.

Police officials and the information media asserted that neo-Nazi agitators had infiltrated the *tifoseria* (loosely organized groups of militant fans) to stir up trouble. Actually, skinheads of both the Roma and the Lazio persuasion have lately been heard shouting profascist and anti-Semitic slogans in the Olympic Stadium.

Political extremism thrives in the subculture of violence and vandalism that has haunted Italian soccer for years in the same way as hooliganism has frequently marred sports events in Britain and other European countries.

Today the *romanisti* "ultras" in the south curve, their traditional habitat in the stadium, were comparatively restrained in their jubilation, just setting off firecrackers and starting a few bonfires. Their hero today was Daniel Fonseca, the Roma center forward who with a splendid assist helped bring about the first goal soon after the game's start, and also scored the second one. The dark, wiry Fonseca is a Uruguayan, one of the many stars of the pampered foreign legion in Italy's professional soccer. Other non-Italians in the field today included a Lazio Croat who, after only a few minutes, suffered a knee injury in a rough tackle and had to be replaced.

Roma's trainer, the white-haired, paunchy Carlo Mazzone, got his share of cheers for a change, after weeks of boos from the fans and condescending criticisms by the sports commentators. His Lazio opposite number, Zdenek Zeman, acknowledged defeat with stoicism; earlier in the current season the Czech "mister" had won general acclaim for the team's successes. Soccer players and fans here refer to their club's coach as *il mister*—a usage going back to the beginning of the twentieth century when association football was first introduced into Italy from England, and the first professional trainers were a Mr. Smith or Mr. Brown.

The disorders in the north curve of the stadium were essentially a battle between Lazio militants and the police. I saw the raging *tifosi* claw at the wire nets that separated them from the other sections and throw detached pieces of seats and other objects into the field while lawmen were keenly swinging their truncheons to tame them.

The damages sustained by the stadium were negligible, compared with the $3.5 million grossed by ticket sales. As usual there were a lot of fake tickets in circulation, too, and at least a few fans who had been victimized managed to get into the stadium anyway.

It was also a great day for the multitudes who play the *Toto-calcio*, the Italian version of soccer pools. The moment the Derby match ended, the computers of the soccer lottery started spinning, and a couple of hours later the sports broadcasts announced that only seven ticket holders in all of Italy had correctly guessed the outcome of the day's thirteen games listed on the pool forms, each winning something like $1.3 million on a stake of as little as two dollars. The majority of players consider themselves soccer experts and try to anticipate what's going to happen in the stadiums on the basis of the recent performance by the various teams. Most pool addicts expected the Lazio to win the Derby.

The official soccer-pool organization pays sizable taxes to the Treasury, and also helps finance Italian sports. Payoffs, however, are richer in the illegal betting systems that mafia groups run—efficiently, I am assured by people who should know. *Totocalcio* forms are filled in at espresso bars and other places until the beginning of the games—2:30 P.M. today throughout Italy. Clandestine bets can be placed with agents of the underground networks, not only in many city neighborhoods but also at the stadium, and winners get their money immediately after the match.

Betting, rows, and shady people at the stadium are nothing new here. The racecourses of ancient Rome teemed with gamblers, fortune-tellers, and prostitutes, contemporary writers tell us. Fans went wild over the feats of such stars as Lacerta (The Lizard), a charioteer who drove for the Red faction, and they applauded the mettle of thoroughbred horses called Coryphaeus (The Leader) or Irpinus (a name denoting southern Italian origin).

At home tonight I reread the pertinent passage of Gibbon's *Decline and Fall of the Roman Empire*: "The profits of a favorite charioteer sometimes exceeded those of an advocate . . . the wages of a disgraceful profession." What would Gibbon have said on learning that an Italian soccer hero earns more than the chief justice of the Constitutional High Court and the president of the republic?

In imperial Rome the original White and Red circus factions were soon complemented by the Greens and the Blues, and the two latter became the Lazio and Roma of the ancient world when, again in Gibbon's words, the populace at the center of the empire "devoted their lives and fortunes to the color which they had espoused." Violent and often bloody disturbances at the race-course were frequent until the sixth century A.D., and the history of medieval Rome is filled with other factional strife.

Today the Derby brought us again a conflict of colors—the Lazio's blue and white against the yellow and purple of the Roma.

December

• Teatime •

DECEMBER 8

Days ago Alexander, an old friend from London, asked me to have tea with him at Babington's in the Spanish Square. He didn't know that December 8 is the Roman Catholic Feast of the Immaculate Conception and a legal holiday here, and I didn't think of it when we set the date for this afternoon. For the last several years the pope has been driven from the Vatican to the Spanish Square in the afternoon of December 8 to pray at the foot of the column carrying a statue of the Virgin Mary; the ceremony today was scheduled for four P.M.—just when my friend and I were to meet.

The Spagna (Spain) subway stop under the Spanish Square was closed all afternoon to prevent overcrowding. As trains were bypassing that stop, I got out at the Piazzale Flaminio and proceeded on foot to the Spanish Square, which I found packed with people. The police would later estimate that thirty thousand persons had gathered there to greet John Paul II. The figure may be slightly exaggerated, but at any rate I had to shoulder toward Babington's on the left flank of the Spanish Stairs.

As I approached our meeting place, I heard hands clapping and cheers. I squeezed onto one of the lower steps of the Spanish Staircase, which was already crowded all the way up, and saw the pontiff in an open black car—not his bulletproof Popemobile—as it turned from the narrow Via de' Condotti toward the south side of the Spanish Square. John Paul II sat alone in the rear, a crimson cape over his white cassock. Four tall security men in dark business suits were walking at either side of the slow-moving vehicle.

A woman behind me said to another, "Look, he has still his hand bandaged." The pope broke the little finger of his right hand when it was caught by a car door several days ago. The Romans always watch the physical condition of their bishop, and have been doing so with morbid fascination ever since John Paul II underwent intestinal and hip surgery during two recent sojourns in the hospital and suffered a series of minor mishaps like that broken finger. Today he seemed fatigued.

The pope left his car in front of the Spanish Embassy to the Holy See, presumably being helped out (although I couldn't see it from where I stood). The embassy facade was illuminated and adorned with purple tapestries hanging from the windows and the front balcony. The flags of Spain, red and gold, and of the papacy, yellow and white, were fluttering from the building. The palazzo has housed the Spanish diplomatic mission to the Vatican for three hundred years and has given its name to the square and to the Spanish Stairs (although that monumental passage was built during 1721–25 with French money).

Since early this morning, Roman civic and church groups, nuns, and private citizens had heaped flowers on the base of the column of Our Lady, in front of the Spanish Embassy; the fire department had sent a ladder to place a wreath of white blossoms on the bronze statue's outstretched right arm. The tall stalk of veined marble, crowned with the Madonna sculpture, was erected on orders from Pope Pius IX to commemorate his proclamation of the dogma of the Virgin Mary's Immaculate Conception on December 8, 1854, exactly 140 years ago today.

Though I left to meet Alexander, I would catch the rest of the ceremony on television later in the evening. The mayor of Rome, with his wife and two children, and other city dignitaries with their families received John Paul in the piazza. The Polish pontiff faced the column, paying silent tribute to the Madonna, then turned around, and, in a brief speech over a public address system, told the crowd in Italian that as a child "in my fatherland" he had felt particular veneration for the Blessed Virgin.

When I arrived at Babington's Tearooms, which I hadn't visited for years, I found the establishment unchanged. Under the white-washed, wood-beamed ceilings there were still the famously uncomfortable chairs with their straight wooden backs, and the little square tables with straw mats. The black-and-white cat, Keeko, had become fat and slow but still cadged handouts from patrons. The middle-aged Italian waitresses, in pink smocks, still looked moody. The pendulum clock was still on the wall, and the curtains were still green and white. The tea, served in green crockery with plenty of extra hot water, was still excellent. The dark wood paneling and other decor may indeed go back to 1883, when Anna Maria Babington and Isabel Cargill opened the place. For added English authenticity my friend ordered scones with our tea.

Babington's is one of the last vestiges of what from the late eighteenth century to the early twentieth was a thriving British enclave in Rome. The Piazza di Spagna was actually an English square during the long period when English lords, poets, painters, and art-loving spinsters spent winters in Rome or inhabited the city permanently as expatriates.

Keats lived, and in 1821 died, in the graceful pink building at the right side of the Spanish Stairs, now the Keats-Shelley Memorial House. Byron at one time was a lodger across the square (at No. 66 Piazza di Spagna), but efforts to create memorial rooms for that hero of Romanticism—or at least to put a plaque on the facade—have remained unsuccessful.

Another holdout of British Rome is the All Saints Anglican Church on the west side of the Via del Babuino, a few blocks from the Spanish Square, where services are held every Sunday and on four weekdays. One Sunday morning during the fifties I experienced a thrill there when a guest from England who had volunteered to sing in the worship service had asked me to be present. As her voice wafted down from the choir loft a shiver ran down my spine, and people in the congregation looked at one another in astonishment. I said to myself, "She's got it!" The timbre of that voice resembled that of the early Maria Callas.

The owner of the voice was a chubby, amiable post office employee from the Midlands who had won a singing contest sponsored by the London *Daily Mail,* and who had been awarded a scholarship in Rome to be coached in operatic roles by a once-famous soprano, Toti Dal Monte. Friends in London had asked me to look after the young woman; I had found a boardinghouse for her and arranged for singing lessons with Miss Dal Monte. After hearing her in the Anglican church I was convinced the young singer was headed for a brilliant career. But she wasn't. She returned to England after having studied arias from *La Forza del*

Destino and other Verdi operas, and what happened then I don't know. The last I heard was that she had rejoined the post office.

A few steps from the Anglican church, on the same side of Via del Babuino, is the Lion Bookshop, a prime purveyor of English-language literature in Rome. It was opened after World War II by the sister of a British journalist colleague of mine together with another Englishwoman. By now, under another management, it functions as an unofficial center of the English-language community in the city, as is shown by its billboard with many notices offering apartments and rooms for rent, language lessons, and baby-sitting services. Despite the Lion Bookshop, the Anglican church, and Babington's, Britons today are a minority among the many foreigners who can always be encountered in this cosmopolitan section of Rome.

No tourist misses the Spanish Square. Close to the column of the Virgin Mary where the pope prayed today are an American Express office and a McDonald's franchise; banks, money exchanges, fashion boutiques, and souvenir shops ring the piazza. The Spanish Stairs, the rococo landmark that theatrically sweeps up to the elegant, twin-towered Church of Trinità dei Monti in 137 steps, has become something of a problem. Young tourists sit on the stone steps and parapets for hours day and night; in warm weather, backpackers try to camp there; sidewalk artists and souvenir vendors do business on the stairs; and panhandlers, pickpockets, drug peddlers, and leather-jacketed rowdies from the outskirts infest it.

The state police keep a permanent guard post in a camper parked in front of Babington's, and the Carabinieri frequently patrol the square by car or on foot. Mounted Carabinieri are often seen in pairs in the piazza, but their presence seems more a photo opportunity for tourists rather than a law-enforcing measure, and the horses soil an area that's already hard to keep clean. Plainclothes agents mingle with the crowds on the Spanish Stairs, yet petty crime, fights, noisy scenes, and other undesirable episodes occur nevertheless.

One recent night a police patrol spotted flames on the landing halfway up the Spanish Stairs and found that a group of young-sters had kindled a fire to boil spaghetti in a large pot. At other times young female tourists have complained about being molested. Local newspapers have for some time charged that the ambiance in the Spanish Square and on the Spanish Steps has deteriorated deplorably. A member of Parliament proposed this week to restrict the public use of the famous staircase, merely per-mitting the passage of pedestrians but fining anyone who sits down or loiters on the steps.

• Gangster Lore •

DECEMBER 10

The police announced today they had captured "the last" member of the Magliana gang. I wouldn't take the claim literally, but there is no doubt that the investigators have worked hard for several years to smash the redoubtable crime organization. Belying the Romans' reputation for easygoing ways (even in delinquency), the bumbling hoods of the Roman film classic *Big Deal on Madonna Street* seemed more typical of local small-time crime than were the ruth-less Magliana gangsters.

The Magliana is a once-malarial strip on the far southern out-skirts of the city between the low hills and the right bank of the Tiber where the river exits from Rome to flow torpidly to the nearby sea.

The Magliana suburb derives its name—similar to the Italian word for mesh (*maglia*)—from a little stream that contributes water from the hillside to the Tiber. A former hunting lodge, now ruined, situated about half a mile north of the motorway and railroad line to Fiumicino, is known as the Villa La Magliana. It was a favorite retreat of Pope Leo X. That Medici pontiff, who reigned in Renaissance splendor from 1513 to 1521, liked to hunt in the Magliana fields and forests, shocking more zealous churchmen by wearing high boots for his strenuous outdoor sport.

When I first saw the district many years ago, the narrow, old highway and the railroad line to the fishing village of Fiumicino traversed it between kitchen gardens, a few decrepit inns, a multitude of shacks, and a scruffy hamlet. Then, real estate developers took over and filled the strip with mean housing.

Soon after the big Fiumicino Airport opened in 1960, a new motor road was built to link it with the center of Rome across the Magliana section. Various large hotels for business travelers and conventioneers sprang up nearby. The area now boasts a golf course, too. Yet shacks and slum housing are still scattered about the neighborhood, which air passengers see on their way to or from Fiumicino Airport but which few Romans know well.

We have been hearing of the Magliana gang for the last twenty years or so. It used to be described as a set of hoodlums—native Romans and immigrants from southern Italy—who were living in the tacky suburban river neighborhood and had graduated from burglaries, thefts, muggings, and holdups to kidnappings and brutal murders. The gang was said to have established control over the district's fences, usurers, drug pushers, and pimps.

What's more, the police soon had worrying evidence that the Magliana thugs were doing special jobs commissioned by Sicilian mafia families and Calabrian and Neapolitan racketeer factions: the Roman gangsters were hiring out as goons for southern-based organized crime. At its peak period in the late eighties, the Magliana gang appeared to have nursed the ambition to become a mafia-type crime syndicate enforcing control of the entire under-world not only in Rome but also in a vast territory around the capital.

Police officials and the local news media would allege Magliana involvement in about any of the unsolved crime myster-ies that appalled Rome during the past several years. A number of presumed operatives of the gang were eventually arrested, one after another, in various police actions. They were tried on diverse charges and sentenced to long prison terms. Evidence presented in court depicted the defendants as hardened, sadistic criminals who tortured their victims before killing them, which until then had been believed to happen only in Sicily.

In 1977 the Magliana gang made headlines nationwide when it kidnapped a sixty-six-year-old Roman nobleman, Duke Massimi-liano Grazioli. The thugs held him consecutively in two secret prisons for a month, extorted a $2.5 million ransom from his fam-ily, and then, instead of freeing the aristocrat, sold him to a Naples camorra gang, which tried to milk his relatives for more money. Eventually the Neapolitans murdered the duke, apparently because he had seen the face of at least one of them and might have been able to identify the man after being released.

The suspect who was arrested earlier this week in a Magliana apartment is Giovanni di Gennaro, nicknamed "Angel Face," age forty-four. The police allege it was he who fingered the wealthy duke as a potential and promising kidnap target, observed his movements, and enabled other members of the gang—who at present are already serving jail sentences—to seize him as he was driving, followed by a bodyguard in a separate car, from his palazzo in Rome to a mansion in the countryside northeast of the city.

The police stated today that "Angel Face" was the eleventh top figure of the Magliana gang to be behind bars. Nearly a hundred alleged members of the big Roman crime organization—some in prison, some free under police surveillance, and a few still at large—are to be tried here next fall.

• St. Peter's Square, a Pine, and a Pope •

DECEMBER 15

A crane lifted a huge Christmas tree from a four-axle truck in St. Peter's Square this morning, and Vatican workers using two white cherry pickers started decorating it with electric candles, colored glass globes, and tinsel. The pine tree, a gift to the pope from Slovakia, had been cut in the Tatra Mountains not far from John Paul II's birthplace, Wadowice, near Kraków in Poland. He is scheduled to revisit those mountains come spring.

The mighty conifer rises now a few yards north of the Egyptian obelisk in the center of the piazza. The granite monolith, devoid of hieroglyphs, is three thousand years old and eighty-two feet high; the tree is almost equally tall and must also be quite old, judging from the trunk, which one can't enclose at its base with one arm alone.

A yuletide tree in front of the greatest church in Christendom is by now customary, but the custom is young, introduced as it was by John Paul II after his election in 1978. The Polish pontiff's desire to see a Christmas tree in St. Peter's Square when he looked out of his windows in the Apostolic Palace caused no little astonishment in the Vatican at the time. Roman churchmen had for decades frowned at the invasion of Roman homes and public places by such trees, denouncing them as pagan symbols. Christmas trees of course had always adorned churches and the homes of churchgoing people as well as railroad stations and town squares in temperate and Nordic countries, including Poland.

The Fascist dictatorship, too, thought the (then nascent) Italian vogue of Christmas trees to be barbaric. The trees became acceptable in the eyes of nationalists only when Mussolini allied himself with Hitler. For some time, at any rate, the church and the Fascists had been in agreement that the traditional, correct Italian way of celebrating the yuletide was with the *presepe*, a miniature nativity scene with the figures of the Holy Family, the shepherds, and the oxen and sheep around the manger, and the Three Wise Men with the star they had followed. Saint Francis of Assisi is pictured in a fresco by Giotto as building such a representation of the manger at Bethlehem. Crèches, often with hand-carved wooden figures, can be found in churches and museums all over Italy, some of them striking by their artistic distinction in their archaic naïveté.

These days, many churches in Rome are taking their crèches out of storerooms and assembling them in naves and side chapels. Many Roman parents used to take their children on a tour of various churches to look at their *presepi;* some still do. A show of a hundred specimens of this old folk-art has just been opened in the art gallery adjoining Santa Maria del Popolo—the church where Martin Luther worshiped during his visit to Rome, 1510–11, long before he broke with the papacy.

In years past, enterprising rectors of some churches here had installed elaborate nativity scenes in which the figures moved and lights twinkled for a few minutes when a coin was dropped in a slot. A few such mechanical crèches can still be seen here and there at this time of the year, but it seems nostalgic oldsters are more interested in them than are the jaded kids of the television and video game era.

To balance the impact of the pagan Christmas tree in St. Peter's Square, the Vatican now also erects a big scenic crèche with life-size figures in front of the obelisk every yuletide. Canvas curtains today were still shrouding the steel-tube skeleton of the structure, which will be unveiled only on Christmas Eve, to remain on display with the tree from the Tatra Mountains until the end of January. The nativity display in St. Peter's Square is like the stage of a theater, and with the obelisk, the Christmas tree, and the facade of the Basilica of St. Peter's as a backdrop, it provides an irresistible setting for a souvenir photo. Although the big crèche was not yet visible this morning, some Japanese tourists still took snapshot after snapshot.

As I was standing in St. Peter's Square surveying the pre-Christmas activity, it suddenly occurred to me that I had parked a jeep in the very same spot almost exactly fifty years earlier. The square, which belongs to the State of Vatican City, is closed to motor traffic, but then it was okay, at least for us, to drive into it. The large inscription THE NEW YORK TIMES on the vehicle's front board was new, but the jeep was old and battered; the Rome bureau of our newspaper had just obtained it as war surplus material from the United States Army.

Rome had been liberated by the Allied forces only six months earlier. I was then a newcomer to the *Times*, but my bureau chief, Herbert L. Matthews, had asked me to arrange a papal audience for a visitor from New York because I happened to know a prelate with good Vatican connections. It took my ecclesiastical friend, monsignor Pietro Ercole from the pope's Vicariat for Rome, only a couple of phone calls to set up an appointment with the pontiff with short notice. Vatican procedures were less rigid then than they are now. Msgr. Ercole, however, warned me: "The Holy Father will see your colleague just for a few minutes. No interview!"

Our visitor was Meyer Berger, a star reporter of our newspaper. I had found him waiting in front of our office in the Via della Mercede a few mornings earlier when I went, as the youngest member of the staff, to open it for the day. Berger was wearing the uniform of an American war correspondent and explained he really should be in Tunis. North Africa had slipped out of the news since the Allied invasions of Italy and France, but the editors in New York had figured that our readers might be interested to learn what was happening then in Tunisia and Algeria and had asked Berger to report from there. Bad weather or some other reason had diverted the military aircraft on which he was traveling to Italy. While Berger was waiting for a flight to Tunis, he thought he might as well interview Pope Pius XII. He didn't know that the pontiff had never granted an interview and wouldn't do so now.

A little before the appointed time for the late-morning audience we drove to St. Peter's Square in the newly acquired office jeep, left it in the piazza, and passed the Bronze Doors. The Swiss Guards, apparently mistaking the slender, middle-aged man in American uniform for a senior officer, presented their halberds, and Berger saluted smartly.

One of various lay attendants hanging out in the corridor behind the Bronze Doors took charge of us and escorted us across the courtyard of Saint Damasus to the Clementine Hall of the Apostolic Palace. On its marble floor several other people, most of them in American, British, Canadian, or French uniforms, were already waiting. We joined the line. Eventually the tall, thin figure of Pius XII in a white cassock appeared from a low side door, accompanied by two Swiss Guards and a black-clad priest. I had never seen the pope so closely, and was impressed by the pallor of his austere, bespectacled face.

It took about fifteen minutes for Pius XII to walk down the line and say a few words to each of his visitors, whose names the priest at his side read from a list. When the pontiff had come to us, Berger bowed deeply, and Pius XII said to him in halting English,

"So you are from the *New York Times*? A great newspaper." Berger straightened up and replied, "It's the greatest, Your Holiness."

As the pope's hieratic manner dissolved into a thin smile, I was struck by the startling resemblance between the two. Had Pius XII worn an American uniform and Berger a white cassock with a white skullcap, nobody present in the hall would have suspected anything wrong.

The pope ended the brief audience saying, again in his accented English, he would like to give his blessing to the *Times* and to all who worked for it. As he raised his thin, seemingly bloodless hand, I, as a Catholic, made the sign of the cross. Berger, who must have felt he too ought somehow to acknowledge the papal benediction, said heartily, "God bless you too, Your Holiness!" Pius XII reacted with what seemed the ghost of a pontifical grin and withdrew with his Swiss Guards and clerical attendant through the little door.

As we walked to our jeep in St. Peter's Square, Berger turned to me and in mock seriousness said, "You know, I must be the first Jew to bless a pope."

• Let's Call 144 •

DECEMBER 21

Regular classes were held in the Visconti High School for a very few days before the Christmas vacation started today, but many other schools in the city, as all over Italy, remained "okkupied" by rebellious students until yesterday, when all went home. I was wrong last month when I thought the protest movement in the schools would soon fizzle out as it had in past years. This time the youthful militants said they were fighting against the nation's antiquated education system, and against a government plan to curtail pension entitlements, although the teenage activists have a long way to retirement. They first must get a job, and then keep working for thirty-five years.

The government, absorbed by political infighting among its own supporters, did virtually nothing to end the student revolt. It neither negotiated with the protesters nor followed hawkish recommendations to order the police into the schools to throw out the "okkupiers."

School administrators assert that the supposed "self-management" caused great damage to many institutions—classrooms and office furniture were wrecked, computers stolen, and walls covered with truculent graffiti. The heavy phone bills that the student squatters ran up in some schools were allegedly caused by long calls to 144 numbers, the code for telephone-sex services.

• *Urbi et Orbi* •

DECEMBER 25

Christmas weather was ideal—almost cloudless and chilly with only a slight northerly breeze this morning, and warm sunshine bathing St. Peter's Square at noon. The pigeons for once had resentfully withdrawn to the roofs because the piazza, which they assiduously work on other days, was filled with people. On the basis of long experience with Vatican crowds I estimated the number of persons who had gathered in the square and on its approaches at fifty thousand, although, as usual, news reports would mention multiples of that figure.

Visitors from the Italian provinces and foreign tourists prevailed among the people in the square, but there were also plenty of Romans, unmistakable because of their broad dialect; many of the latter were men with children—their womenfolk had remained at home to prepare the Christmas meal, which here is an overabundant late lunch or a very early dinner. As always, vendors were hawking toy balloons just outside the piazza, and a few kids, who, minutes earlier, had been whining "I wanna balloon!" inevitably let go of them by accident or on purpose, and watched them slowly float into the blue, drifting in the breeze toward the pines on the crest of the Janiculum hill south of the square.

Latin Americans (it's summer traveling time in their part of the world) and Japanese were conspicuous in the cosmopolitan crowd. The canvas screens had been lifted last night from the large crèche in front of the obelisk and the tall Christmas tree from Slovakia: it was as if the curtain of a theatrical stage had at last rung up. This morning, people lined up to take pictures of each other in front of the nativity scene. The mood in the piazza was that of a folklore happening for the benefit of mass tourism rather than of a religious event. The unoriginal thought occurred to me that a Christian desirous of a mystical experience had better seek it in some remote village church, perhaps in the hills of Umbria or in the Alps.

I followed parts of the pope's midnight mass in St. Peter's on television last night when viewers could plainly see—better than people actually in the congregation—that John Paul II looked tired and walked slowly, with evident difficulty, and was probably in pain. The little finger of his right hand was still bandaged.

Before the pontiff appeared on the central loggia of St. Peter's at noon today, a company of the Swiss Guard in their yellow, red, and blue Renaissance outfits with halberds and shiny archaic helmets had drawn up at one side of the square, close to the basilica's facade. Facing them was a company of Italian Carabinieri in their gala uniforms, with tall blue-and-red tufts on their eighteenth-century bicornes.

Just as the clocks marked twelve noon, John Paul, in his heavy liturgical vestments, a white-and-gold miter on his head, stepped out on the balcony, flanked by two white-mitered cardinals (one of them an Indian) and other prelates in black. The band of the Carabinieri struck up the first few bars of the official papal hymn, a triumphal tune by Gounod, and the Swiss Guard reciprocated with the first notes of the Italian national anthem.

The crowd in the piazza cheered and waved handkerchiefs, and after a few minutes the pope started speaking into the microphone that a priest was holding in front of him. His address, in Italian, was in large part devoted to praising family values, pegged on the biblical story of the infant Jesus with the Virgin Mary and Saint Joseph in Bethlehem. At the end of his ten-minute speech the pope called for peace in Bosnia, the Caucasus, Rwanda and Burundi, the Sudan, Algeria, and the Holy Land.

Then came what Vatican officials and the Italian information media never seem to tire of calling *urbi et orbi,* the papal blessing, although the three words are not in the actual Latin benediction formula. The curial play on words, of questionable taste as most puns, means the invocation of heavenly benevolence for "the city [of Rome] and the world." The Italian television and radio networks reiterated the trite *urbi et orbi* in every newscast during the remainder of the day, and local newspapers will unavoidably take up the cliché when they are to come out again the day after tomorrow at the end of their two-day vacation.

The crowd in the square applauded again as it would have after a tenor's bravura aria at the opera. The papal outdoor performance concluded with John Paul's wish for a "blessed Christmas" in fifty-three different languages, including Albanian, Kiswahili, and Vietnamese. The polyglot exercise, with yet another couple of idioms added every year, has become something of an embarrassment even to devout Roman Catholics. Pope Paul VI introduced the pontifical speaking in tongues at Christmas and Easter, although he spoke only Italian and French really fluently and, as well as he could, read the brief messages in other languages from scripts prepared by aides. His successor, John Paul I, who reigned for only thirty-three days, didn't have time to follow his example, but John Paul II took up the innovation with relish.

The Polish pope is a linguist, but of course he doesn't sound equally sure in all the eight languages with which he is acquainted. In his English well-wishing today he pronounced Christ as "Kreest." His Spanish is good and drew loud cheers from Hispanics in the piazza today. But what sense does it make for the pope to struggle through sentences in Finnish, Japanese, and Urdu from the loggia of St. Peter's? Latin was once sufficient for popes.

When John Paul II had withdrawn from the loggia, I heard a little girl near me ask her father in Italian, "What will he get for dinner today?" The man replied: "Oh, I guess pork sausages, that sort of thing. The Holy Father is a Pole, you know, and they like fatty stuff." Food seemed to be very much on the minds of many other people in the crowd, and most of them dispersed quickly after the papal blessing. St. Peter's Square was soon left to the pigeons again and to pale tourists from northern countries, who spread out on the steps of the colonnades to luxuriate in the Roman midday sun.

The afternoon was exceptionally quiet, with street traffic at a minimum. Foreigners were at a loss as to what to do besides stroll, what with public transport at a standstill and museums, stores, and theaters all closed. Even most restaurants and espresso bars were shuttered.

Some of the Romans I know have left for ski resorts or are spending the holidays in glamourous places like Positano, Portofino, Paris, Monte Carlo, or the Maldives. Others are celebrating with relatives in family reunions that will go on until late, most likely helping themselves to *panettone* (Milan cake) and sweet wine while playing *tombola*, a kind of family bingo.

You can avoid *tombola* (which gives me the creeps) at Christmas, as we did, but you can't escape *panettone*. The cake, deep brown on the tall outsides and egg-yellow inside, studded with raisins and candied fruits and flavored with mysterious additives, is a northern yuletide sweet that has long conquered all of Italy. Today it is turned out industrially by large food companies (the biggest of them state-controlled, but soon to be privatized) and by confectioners all over the country, and is marketed this time of the year in fancy cardboard boxes by the millions.

A *panettone* is loaded with chemicals to avoid spoilage; this is a sensible precaution, because you are likely to get so many one-kilo (2.2-pound) versions of the standard cake as Christmas or New Year gifts that you cannot possibly eat them all in just a few days. But you are always reluctant to throw them out. After the holiday period, stores will again, as every year, offer cut-rate, unsold *panettoni*, two for the price of one, and many Romans will eat them for breakfast and dessert until March. I am sure the pope, too, had a *panettone* today, together with Polish sweets.

• Cat Plague •

DECEMBER 28

A wave of infectious feline diseases, a cluster of syndromes apparently related to leukemia, is decimating the city's cat population. The newspapers darkly write about a "cats' AIDS," hastening to reassure readers that human beings don't have to fear contagion. City Hall's new delegate in charge of animal rights, Monica Cirinà, confirms that many cats are sick, but she deplores the press campaign on the ground that it might cause a panic among Rome's innumerable cat lovers and prompt a feline pogrom.

Tabbies live in hundreds of thousands of households here. A contessa in my neighborhood who owns a neutered female put her under quarantine as of this morning: Tigre (tigress) is no longer allowed to roam the grassy plot behind her villa. "I am afraid she may be infected by one of the poor stray cats," the contessa explained. She reported to me that Tigre, who despite her name is far from fierce, was puzzled and sullen about being confined to the apartment in such sunny weather as is cheering us today.

The many stray cats in my section of Rome seemed unconcerned this morning, sitting languorously on the roofs of parked cars (their favorite place for rest and observation) and waiting for handouts. Cats without a permanent home have always been a conspicuous feature of this city. According to a recent veterinary census, there are 200,000 of them in Rome at present, most of which live in one of many feline colonies while others prowl neighborhoods as loners.

Nobody dares estimate the strength of the city's underground army of rats, although it isn't all that clandestine. Rome's cats— both the pampered majority living in homes, often on store-bought kitty food, and the scrawny, street-wise strays—seem to have long given up hunting the rodents.

For their livelihood, the stray cats depend almost exclusively on the charity of a *gattara*. A specific Roman character, a *gattara* is a woman, often elderly, who has chosen to take care of one of the many tribes of homeless cats scattered around the city, delivering to it a daily supply of fish heads, chopped liver expressly bought at the butcher's, or spaghetti and meat sauce. The idiom lacks a term *gattaro* for male benefactors of the cat republics, although I have seen a few of them in action, too.

I myself occasionally leave the remains of a chicken dinner or other goodies for the cats living under unused café tables and in the concrete pipes stacked, apparently forever, behind an espresso bar near where I live. I try not to be seen by the attendant of the adjacent garage who, I suspect, is an ailurophobe. When I come home at night, the paper in which I had wrapped my contribution to cat welfare is always licked clean, and I put it in the Dumpster outside the espresso establishment.

I wouldn't qualify, though, for membership in the *gattara* community because the feline dinners that I provide are far from regular, and also because I don't know the cats living between the garage and the rear of the espresso bar very well, and they probably don't know me. (Yet the other day one stared at me and meowed softly.)

When a genuine *gattara* is still thirty steps away from the spot where she usually lays out the day's meal, a dozen or so cats are already assembled, and others come running and leaping. The *gattara* fondly watches the animals as they devour their food, talks to regulars, and exhorts newcomers not to be greedy. The cats jostle to get the best scraps but rarely fight. The *gattara* knows better than to stroke her favorites because, alas, they are plagued with fleas.

A young research assistant I know, Elisabetta, started feeding stray cats in the large courtyard of her building near the Tiber. She eventually took one, then another—a blind one—home; she had them cleaned of vermin and purged of parasites, and she has become their slave. Both sleep in her bed and often awaken her at daybreak.

Another *gattara* is Teresa, a part-time maid, who almost every day takes the bus to the distant Prima Porta Cemetery to visit the grave of her only child, who died at the age of two many years ago. Teresa always takes scraps with her to feed the cats that live in the cemetery, and it isn't quite clear—probably not even to herself—whether she takes the long bus rides to and from the cemetery for the long-dead little boy or feels responsible for the cemetery cats.

The city's animal rights deputy, Mrs. Cirinà, who is a married lawyer in her mid-thirties, has herself taken several cats into her and her patient husband's childless home and is known around City Hall as *La Gattara*, although she also concerns herself with several other species of the animal kingdom, including the starlings.

Until recently the best-known feline colonies could be observed around the Pantheon; among the foundations of the ruined temples from ancient Rome's republican era below the level of the Largo di Torre Argentina; in the substructures of Capitol Hill; in the Colosseum; and in other archeological sites. But as banks, corporate headquarters, and sundry new offices are squeezing many families out of their homes in the historic center, its resident population shrinks, and so does the number of *gattare*—and of cats. With the householders and their pets, many of the city's unplaced cats have relocated to outlying sections and suburbs and have established new settlements like the one near my home. They have found old and new *gattare* to feed them.

Early this year the vast but usually meek sorority of Roman *gattare* became rebellious when the national Parliament appeared to have nothing better to do than attempt to regulate their activities. An amendment to a draft bill on pets passed by the Agricultural Committee of the Chamber of Deputies would have obliged persons who habitually feed stray cats to register with the municipal authorities; they would be fined, under the proposed legislation, if they didn't pick up the unsightly and unsanitary remains of the feline dinners they deliver. The Society for the Protection of Animals and environmental groups protested on the ground that the proposed licensing of *gattare* would cause a feline famine in Rome. The amendment died in Parliament.

Romans and cats have been partners since antiquity, although at the time of Julius Caesar the animals were still an exotic rarity in the city. The first of them had been brought to republican Rome by Phoenician traders from Egypt, where the mice hunters had long been domesticated as defenders of the granaries. Under the pharaohs, cats attained the status of minor divinities. After the Romans conquered the Nile country the cat population on the Tiber grew; one can imagine the outrage and jealousy of the Maltese lapdogs that refined Roman ladies loved to coddle.

Feline life in Rome through the centuries wasn't untroubled. During the Middle Ages, cats, especially if they had the misfortune of being black, often suffered persecution as presumed disguises of Satan—the semideities of pharaonic Egypt had become devilish monsters in the city of the popes. I like to imagine that even then some tender-hearted *gattara* like Elisabetta hid and fed one of the calumniated and harassed animals.

Toward the end of World War II when food was scarce in Nazi-occupied Rome the species seemed to vanish. In the trattoria, on being offered rabbit as plat du jour, savvy patrons would walk into the kitchen to check on the slaughtered animal's ears to make sure they weren't going to dine on a short-eared street cat.

January

• Forbidden Fireworks •

The restaurant with the most expensive fixed-price New Year's Eve supper was the refurbished Roof Garden of the Cavalieri Hilton Hotel on the Monte Mario, a few hundred yards above where I live: $365 per person at yesterday's lira–dollar exchange rate, a little champagne included. Prices in the many other establishments that staged special affairs last night were more moderate; as far as

I could gather from a few telephone calls this afternoon, all those places appear to have been well patronized.

There is clearly a lot of money around, although a new wave of tax and price increases will go into effect tomorrow. The information media of course speak of a "New Year sting." Newspapers will cost eight percent more; telephone rates are to rise by four percent; television fees are to go up, as are motor tolls, automobile and sales taxes, and health service contributions.

My wife and I spurned the ready-made restaurant and night-club celebrations and did what hundreds of thousands of other Romans did—awaited the new year in familiar company at the home of some friends. The custom in Rome on such occasions is to bring substantial hostess gifts, the minimum being a bottle of pricy bubbly.

We were eighteen people, including a few excited children, in a penthouse apartment near the Via Cassia on the northern outskirts. Though we had been told to expect nothing but a very simple meal, it turned out to be far from frugal. Cold cuts and black olives were offered as appetizers, followed by meat-stuffed tortellini in a hot consommé. Then came the obligatory New Year's dish, *zampone* with lentils. *Zampone* means pig's trotter and is a specialty of the Emilia region, particularly of Parma and Modena, eaten nationwide this time of the year. Today it's almost never a real pig's foot but usually an industrially produced plump sausage filled with fatty, spicy meat. Before being served hot, the *zampone* is long boiled and in the process loses some, but not all, of its fat; a couple of thin slices will do for most appetites. The lentils are mandatory with the *zampone* because, as everybody knows, they symbolize coins, promising plenty of money during the twelve months ahead.

For dessert we had the inevitable *panettone*. We also ate the very last grapes of the season, prescribed for New Year's Eve for a reason that nobody has ever been able to explain to me. The children bit off chunks of *torrone*, which is a marble-hard, sweet stick of almonds, nuts, chocolate, honey, and sugar, while most of the adults, fearing to risk a tooth or two, preferred an apple or a tangerine. There was a lot to drink.

We had heard the New Year's message that the head of state delivered over all Italian television channels at 8:30 P.M. This New Year's Eve, people were more strongly interested in what the nation's president had to say because the government had resigned just before Christmas, and for the first time in its history the Italian republic was going through a cabinet crisis—its fifty-second in fifty years—at yuletide.

Predictably, I was asked how I, the foreigner, was judging the Italian situation, and as usual I replied that it wasn't my business to venture opinions about the domestic affairs of my host country. Some of the others in our party, however, were less reticent, and a lively discussion about Italian politics developed. The children were bored until one woman said, Let's play *tombola*. Now it was my turn for being bored.

As midnight approached, our host, who runs an art gallery, sneaked out onto the terrace. We soon heard a string of firecrackers going off, causing the glass door and the windows to rattle and the children to yell with delight. The kids were about to rush out too, but the women checked them—"It's dangerous, you may get killed!" All around the neighborhood a firestorm of sparklers, rockets, Roman candles, and what sounded like veritable bombs broke out, punctuated by unmistakable shots from guns and automatics. It's the traditional way of greeting the new year in Italy. Under a slight drizzle the night lit up for at least ten minutes, and thunderous booms were heard as if enemy air squadrons were bombing the city.

As every year, the police had seized several tons of illegal fireworks during the last few weeks; yet in our neighborhood market on the Via Andrea Doria, for instance, one could buy big crackers, barely concealed under heads of greens and bushels of fennel. There were also official warnings against the old custom of marking the transition from one year to the next with gunpowder. To no avail: Rome, like cities, towns, and villages up and down the country, erupted again in an orgy of pyrotechnics at midnight.

Our host had quickly come inside again after setting off his token quota of the nationwide craze, and he broke out two bottles of champagne, which yielded a glass for every adult in the room and a small sip for the bigger children. While we cheered, clinked glasses, and hugged and kissed, we heard the wail of an ambulance and meaningfully looked at one another: the ineradicable New Year's follies had meant harm to somebody in the vicinity.

This morning the news broadcasts sounded like battle bulletins. Rome radio announced that the "stupid and criminal" custom of ushering in the new year with unauthorized fireworks had caused injuries to more than a hundred persons in the capital alone, and to many more in the rest of the country. Children had been blinded or lost a hand; in Apulia two little girls had been killed by stray bullets in two separate incidents that oddly occurred in the same area at midnight. The hospitals were busy almost everywhere, and quite a few of the New Year's Eve casualties were reported to be in critical condition.

Rome's city administration bravely tried last night to neutralize the Romans' gusto for do-it-yourself pyrotechnics, inviting the citizenry to a big fireworks display, organized by professionals with all necessary safeguards on the Pincio belvedere. Below, in the Piazza del Popolo, a large crowd watched the show after listening to a concert of golden oldies, played by the massed force of no fewer than fifty grand pianos that had been carted into the square, and viewing clips of film classics on a giant screen. The tune "Singing in the Rain" fittingly accompanied a series of sprinkles, but the wet weather didn't deter the thousands of Romans who had been lured into the open; they might otherwise have done dangerous mischief on their own balconies and terraces or fired shots out of their windows.

Before my first New Year's Eve in Rome I was warned to be off the streets around midnight or, if I were in the open, to repair to a covered passageway or other shelter. The custom then was not only to set off firecrackers but especially to throw old pots and pans, damaged crockery, burned-out lightbulbs and other useless objects out of the windows. In the morning of January 1 the sidewalks and streets were littered with debris; sherds and glass splinters caused flat tires; and the sanitation department had their work cut out for them.

A friend of mine who had parked his car on the Via Flaminia before going to a New Year's party later found the vehicle's roof pushed in by a cluster of empty wine bottles that had been tied together and flung out of an upper-floor window. Another year somebody near where I then lived threw a toilet bowl into the street. During the last several New Year's Eves the cascades of wreckage out of windows have gratifyingly become a mere trickle, while the passion for big bangs at midnight continues unabated.

Another tradition, started only after World War II, also remains alive. At ten o'clock this chilly morning three men jumped into the Tiber from the parapet of the Cavour Bridge and quickly swam to the Tulli Baths; a float was tied up at the right bank a little downstream where they could dry themselves and get dressed. One of the trio was an Algerian. The river-jumping feat was first performed during the 1950s by a Dutch expatriate calling himself "Mr. O.K.," who was a Roman street character.

The New Year plunge into the Tiber, which always draws a few news photographers, is daunting not so much because of the bridge's height—some thirty feet—or the cold water, but because of river pollution. The Tiber carries sickening quantities of un-treated sewage and industrial waste from upstream; bathing in the river has long been prohibited. The old Tulli establishment is nev-ertheless still in business, but only for sunbathing in the warm months, when diehard habitués during their lunch break hurry from their jobs in the city center to the float to build up their tan and have a snack near the smelly river.

• A Benign Witch •

JANUARY 6

My obligatory stroll last night with a teenage visitor from Milan was to the Piazza Navona to take in the *Befana* fun. Susanna declared that the Roman happening was not to be missed; *Befana* is also celebrated in Milan as it is elsewhere in Italy, but the real thing, she had heard, was in the Piazza Navona.

She didn't know, and I had to explain to her, that the word *Befana* is a corruption of *Epiphany*, the name of the Christian feast day commemorating the message to the Magi and the gentile world that the newborn Jesus was the son of God. Susanna, our guest, asked "And where does the witch come in?" Good question.

In a curious linguistic sleight of hand the Romans long ago transformed the Greek term *epiphany* (manifestation) into the earthy-sounding word *Befana* and thought up a witch of that name. Or maybe the witch wasn't an outright invention but a character of the pre-Christian pantheon of supernatural beings. Roman chil-dren at any rate have for centuries been told that the witch *Befana* rides across the sky on a broomstick, carrying a bag, the night before January 6; she enters houses and apartments unobserved and puts things into the stockings hung up for her. Good kids get candy and toys, whereas naughty ones will find coal in their stockings.

At Epiphany, Roman children expected the *Befana's* offerings—an allusion to the gold, frankincense, and myrrh that the Wise Men brought to Bethlehem—long before they started to get Christmas gifts. The *Befana* is older and more deeply rooted in local folklore than is Santa Claus. Cultural influences from northern Europe and the United States, lately reinforced by movies, television, and advertising, have popularized Christmas giving in Rome and in the rest of Italy. The result is that little Romans (and many adults too) expect presents twice within less than two weeks.

Although the witch *Befana* may disappoint unruly kids by filling their stockings with coal and ashes, she is generally pictured as benevolent. Roman dialect nevertheless applies the term *befana* to ugly or nasty old women, and even to unappealing young ones.

I had to take Susanna to the Piazza Navona because thousands of Romans flock there the night before the feast of Epiphany for revelry and impulse purchases at the outdoor market that is held in the square from before Christmas to the end of Italy's extra-long yuletide season. On the way I told our guest that when she was a small girl in the 1980s the government tried to abolish Epiphany as a national holiday because it felt Italians were taking too many days off from work. The idea was, if you want to celebrate *Befana* do it on the Sunday closest to January 6. However, a nationwide outcry prompted the authorities to restore Epiphany to the official roster of holidays. One consequence is that, as before, millions of Italians consider the period from December 23 to January 7 an unbroken vacation and stay away from their jobs. This year's calendar offers an extra bonus: today, Epiphany, is a Friday, and many people who haven't been working since the day before Christmas Eve will start again only Monday, January 9.

Susanna had said she could go alone to the Piazza Navona as she knew how to get there, but her parents in Milan, whom we consulted by phone, insisted she must be accompanied. It was a good thing, because small bands of youths in leather jackets had come from the suburbs to roam in the crowded piazza and engage in horseplay. The night was chilly, the sky clear; the witch's broomstick ride would be smooth.

Stands displaying sweets, toys, cameras, electronic gadgets, T-shirts, sportswear, shoes, comic books, and other merchandise lined the oblong piazza. There were shooting galleries and refreshment booths, and the cafés around the square were thronged. A merry-go-round close to Bernini's Fountain of the Rivers at the center was turning to the shrill sounds of a mechanical organ. A tall Christmas tree nearby reminded me of a scene that occurred here in December: Two men dressed up as Santa Clauses started a fight in the Piazza Navona over who was entitled to stand in front of the Church of Sant' Agnese, apparently a privileged spot. To the delight of bystanders, the two Santas bearded each other in a shoving and pushing match. A policeman eventually separated the disreputable pair.

My young guest laughed when I told her about the two, but she was much less interested in what I, rather pedantically, wanted her to know about the history of one of Rome's loveliest squares: that its elongated shape still betrays its past as a racecourse and a stadium under the Emperor Domitian; that the baroque church on its west side, where the two Santas had been scuffling, rises at the spot of Saint Agnes's supposed martyrdom at the beginning of the fourth century; and that the piazza at times was flooded to create an artificial lake for mock naval battles (hence its name *navona*). "It's now a choice address in Rome," I said. "Step back and look up at the luxurious penthouses that architects have put on top of the ancient buildings as pads for Milanese tycoons who come to the capital every now and then."

Susanna wanted a stick with spun sugar, a treat she claimed she had never had when she was little, and we wandered around the piazza. We returned home around midnight and slept late this morning, missing a parade of make-believe Magi with attendants costumed as ancient Roman legionnaires that moved from the city center to St. Peter's Square. A group of Green movement activists instead marched to the prime minister's office, the Palazzo Chigi, and placed a symbolic load of coals in front of it as a sign that, according to them, the government isn't doing enough for the protection of the environment and therefore deserves the witch's displeasure.

Tomorrow, Saturday, quite a few Romans will line up before nine A.M. outside apparel and fashion stores that have announced post-holiday sales. Their publicity promises price cuts of up to 70 percent, but few people are fooled—only articles that have proved to be a drag on the market will be offered really cheap. Yet many items will cost 10 to 20 percent less than they did before Christmas, enough of an incentive to get out of bed early for a change and go on a shopping expedition. Susanna, who took the afternoon train to Milan today, will have two busy days before her, as school will at last start again on Monday, and she hasn't done any of her holiday homework assignments.

• Queen of Heaven Jail •

JANUARY 11

Dark blue police vans are taking scores of prisoners from the moldy Regina Coeli jail on the right Tiber embankment to correctional facilities in the neighborhood of Rome. It's high time. Health Minister Raffaele Costa inspected the grim complex between the river and the green slope of the Janiculum, close to the Vatican, last month and pronounced it a public hazard.

The minister threatened he would order closure of the over-crowded prison unless conditions were improved and the number of inmates quickly reduced by 50 percent.

Regina Coeli means Queen of Heaven, the lingering name of a church dedicated to the Virgin Mary that once rose in the area. The adjacent monastery was transformed into a jail by the papal government; the Italian state took it over after the nation's unifica-tion in the nineteenth century and built additional cell blocks in a fanlike pattern. Most cells lack heat, and in the summer there is lit-tle ventilation. Sanitation is primitive. The entire jail is malodor-ous, as the health minister couldn't fail to notice the moment he crossed the main gate.

For the judicial authorities and for attorneys, however, the location of the prison is advantageous. Magistrates who have to question arrested suspects, and lawyers wanting to confer with inmates, can dash to the Via della Lungara, where the main entrance is, and be back in their offices in a couple of hours or less. More than half of the prison inmates are defendants awaiting trial—usually for months, sometimes much longer.

The jail's site is also convenient for the relatives of inmates who have visiting permits or want to send packages containing food or, maybe, a clean shirt. There are also secret ways of getting in touch with inmates. Regina Coeli spreads at the northern edge of the motley Trastevere section, where lower-middle-class families live side by side with artists, diplomats like my new friends of the French Embassy, intellectuals, and wealthy expatriates. In the neighborhood you will always find somebody who can provide a not-quite-legal channel to prison personnel and inmates. An old, sardonic adage in the city has it that one isn't a genuine Roman if one hasn't done time in Regina Coeli. At present, however, many inmates are actually recent and often clandestine immigrants from underdeveloped countries who probably will be expelled from Italy after sentencing, and who may soon be back.

Whenever I find myself near Regina Coeli I am reminded of a jarring occurrence involving the old jail that I witnessed soon after Rome's liberation from Nazi rule. Herbert L. Matthews, then chief correspondent of the *New York Times* in Rome, and I were driving along the Tiber when we were engulfed by a wildly shouting mob. To our horror we saw a man being pushed into the river from the middle of a bridge near which we had been forced to stop. The man, who was bleeding from head injuries, came up from the water and began to swim downstream. Two or three youngsters broke away from the crowd on the bridge, ran down to a floating bathing establishment—not the Tulli Baths—tied up at the right riverbank, got hold of a rowboat, followed their victim in the sluggish river, and finished him off with furious oar blows.

It took us some time to find out that the slain man had been the director of Regina Coeli and that his name was Carretta. The Nazis had kept their prisoners and hostages separated from common criminals in the jail's cell block No. 6. One story had it that an ex-detainee freed after the Allied conquest of Rome had come to get even with Carretta; another version was that the prison director had been walking on the embankment and had been recognized by former inmates. Carretta, at any rate, was soon surrounded by people who inveighed at him and started pummeling him; he attempted to escape his tormentors and was chased and severely beaten before being thrown from the bridge.

Days later, former prisoners who had not taken part in the lynching came forward to testify that Carretta had not been particularly cruel, had been a correction officer for many years, and in some instances had shown himself to be humane. On the other hand, they said, he may have assisted the Gestapo in selecting death candidates when the Nazis demanded hundreds of men to be shot in reprisal for a bomb attack on a marching column of SS police in Rome's center on March 23, 1944. In that action thirty-one Germans were killed, and on direct orders from Hitler 335 Italian hostages were shot by the Gestapo in a tufa cave on the old Ardeatine Road on the city's southern outskirts.

The slaying of the Regina Coeli director was one of the very few episodes of major violence after Rome's liberation. Matthews cabled a long report to our newspaper. "This story will make the front page," he told me, "but I would have preferred not to see it happen."

• Cabinet Crisis •

JANUARY 13

A ritual is unfolding that is as Roman as are *Befana* or a Vatican consistory, only much longer and more complicated: Italy is once again going through a government crisis. My friend Massimo, the Milan architect who is a freshman member of Parliament, is quite busy these days. He is one of several thousands of players (though a minor one) in the current political charade—senators, deputies, high dignitaries, support staffs, "briefcase carriers," journalists, television crews, and characters whose roles are hard to define but may be crucial behind the scenes.

The all-too-familiar show has been enacted, with few variations, fifty-three times during the last fifty years; an Italian government on average lasts less than a year. The setting is always the same: the Renaissance and baroque palaces of the head of state and the two houses of Parliament, the Palazzo Chigi from which Italy is supposed to be governed, other official buildings, the offices of the many political parties and their subfactions, and the restaurants in the city center where much of the maneuvering is done over late lunches and long-drawn-out dinners.

The small crowds that often gather in front of the Quirinal Palace, the official residence of the president of the republic, and the Palazzo Chigi are made up mainly of visitors from the provinces, eager to watch firsthand the comings and goings of the politicos whom they have so often seen on television. A few foreign tourists too are always attracted by what seems to them unusual activity. Most Romans however are blasé about the hectic crisis choreography. They mutter sarcastic comments or ripe imprecations whenever the dark blue official limousines, preceded by police cars with sirens at full blast and roof lights flashing, plow through traffic.

The natives should instead appreciate all that agitation. Politics and the government (regardless of whether Italy happens to have one or doesn't) in fact constitute a major local industry, like the Vatican and the tourist trade, in a city that is neither a manufacturing center nor a star performer in the communications or financial services departments. Since the Roman political-bureaucratic establishment handles the state budget, a substantial portion of the revenue is being spent locally.

The current efforts to set up a new government have been going on for the last three weeks; the prime minister resigned just before Christmas because his parliamentary majority had collapsed. Since then he and his ministers have supposedly been acting as a caretaker administration, but of course no real governing is being done. State functionaries routinely run the creaking bureaucratic machinery, leaving any strategic decisions to whomever will be their next department chief. Foreign governments and businesses appear to be puzzled by the Italian situation; the international quotations of the lira have plummeted.

Since Christmas, Italian television audiences have been treated to tedious daily newscasts showing, once again, politicians emerging from meetings with the president of the republic and making statements in language that seems to be in code. The head of state has twice seen all party leaders, one after another, in the stylized ballet called "consultations." Each Sunday night the news broadcasts have announced a "decisive week," which would turn out to be inconclusive, and the media every day reported "convulsive" political activity. What is really convulsive is the city's traffic. The restaurants frequented by the honorable members of Parliament and their hangers-on look placid enough.

This afternoon the president of the republic at last asked the treasury minister of the outgoing cabinet to try to form government No. 53 since the end of World War II. The premier-designate, who until last year was director general of the Bank of Italy, is a Florentine, a financial expert, and a socialite with a rich wife; he has no political background but is well known in international financial circles. Now it's his turn to try to cobble together majorities in both houses of Parliament and come up with a list of ministers. Should he fail, the head of state would have to start another choreographic round of consultations before picking the next candidate for the premiership. New nationwide elections later this year are a possibility, although the last ones were held less than nine months ago. Rome's political industry is in a boom cycle.

• Opera Gala •

JANUARY 15

The 115-year-old Roman opera house has lately lost much of its former prestige owing to its spotty artistic record, its financial woes, and its cranky staff. There were stories that musicians were listening to soccer broadcasts on their portable radios during orchestra rehearsals. Once, partisans of Verdi and Wagner battled in the galleries when the lyric art inflamed passions; at later times the young Herbert von Karajan led the opera house's orchestra; Maria Callas at the height of her career walked out in the middle of a performance of *Norma* because the claque had irritated her, leaving Italy's president, Giovanni Gronchi, baffled in the royal box and other members of the audience clamoring for their money back. There is no longer such excitement. Famous conductors and star singers have lately refused engagements at the Teatro dell'Opera.

One of the reasons adduced for the decline is the impact of television and rock music. Italy's greatest living composer, Goffredo Petrassi, who at the age of ninety is as lucid as ever, said before the new season that the Roman opera house should be closed altogether: "Everybody must go home, from the doorman to the manager. If they have been able to do this in Paris, it can be done here too."

Nevertheless, the Roman opera season opened last night with a $1.4 million production of Hector Berlioz's *Benvenuto Cellini*, and the gala, despite the customary overtones of bickering and intrigue, was a gratifying success. It demonstrated that the long-ailing Teatro dell'Opera still can present a lavish show.

The Berlioz work is 157 years old and is set in Renaissance Rome—yet astonishingly this is its first performance here. The belated premiere was said to symbolize a renewed commitment to the Roman opera house. The national government coughed up $12.5 million to pay the institution's most pressing debts; nine months ago a respected Trieste music expert, Giorgio Vidusso, was hired as the new Rome opera manager. The hope was to alter the course of the institution's checkered history. It wouldn't be an easy task. In fact, the opening gala almost didn't happen.

Four of the seven unions representing the opera house's personnel threatened to strike last week, thus postponing or cancelling the *Benvenuto Cellini* premiere. The Italian operatic world is rife with such complications; the august La Scala Opera House in Milan too faces regular strike threats before the beginning of each season. In the case of the Roman institution, the mayor stepped in just in time to negotiate a provisional settlement with the unions. The labor disputes were over nine redundant firemen and fifty-one part-time workers who wanted staff positions; somehow, they were all bought off.

From our eighty-dollar seats yesterday we could see Vidusso's predecessor, Giampaolo Cresci, in a stage box. A genial former public relations man who publicly admitted he lacked any musical background, he was widely criticized during his brief tenure for extravagantly squandering the opera house's slim resources on such frills as a new sugar-white lobby decor, operetta-style uniforms for the ushers, and a parade of circus elephants in Rome's streets to publicize an *Aida* production.

Cresci took Italian-American composer Giancarlo Menotti as his musical director, but the Teatro dell'Opera continued foundering. Both Menotti and Cresci were soon dismissed.

Last night's gala was scheduled to start at seven o'clock, but at that hour the theater was still half empty. The conductor, John Nelson, appeared in the pit at 7:15, the orchestra struck up the overture, and for the next twenty minutes of the music and stage action latecomers were admitted, causing considerable annoyance by fussily looking for their seats and squeezing through the rows of spectators who had arrived earlier. Punctuality is not a Roman virtue, and the Teatro dell'Opera isn't Bayreuth; nor is Maestro Nelson a Toscanini, who would suspend the music if people were let in after he had started conducting.

The applause after the first act of *Benvenuto Cellini* was well deserved, but its nature and length proved that, as always, the claque was present in force. The house, at any rate, was full by then, but I suspected that many of the women in long dresses and black-tied men hadn't paid for their good seats; politicians, high functionaries, and their families have always obtained free opera tickets. Rome's mayor and his wife and a few other state and municipal worthies graced the former royal box.

The paparazzi worked the lobby and corridors before the performance, and during the long intermissions they crowded around show business and television personages, who more than willingly posed for pictures. I recognized various foreign ambassadors, but as far as I could see few members of the Roman nobility were in the audience. The local aristocrats—all those princes, dukes, marquesses, counts, and barons—never cared much for cultural events.

After the maneuvering and quarrels of the last few weeks, the Teatro dell'Opera presented a creditable rendition of an exacting work that involved its entire staff together with such foreign guests as the conductor and the principal singers. The Australian soprano Deborah Riedel in the part of Teresa, Cellini's girlfriend, earned much applause not generated by the claque. David Kuebler in the title role, though not dazzling by his voice, gave a competent performance. The singing was in French, inevitably with a variety of accents.

What really made the success of the evening was its visual richness. The director, Gigi Proietti, who is a popular actor and sometime restaurateur, and the fashion designer Quirino Conti, responsible for the stage sets and costumes, created a fantastic sixteenth-century Rome; sticklers for historical accuracy might have contended that what was shown was far more in a baroque than in a Renaissance vein. A Roman carnival scene in the first act populated the stage with a hundred grotesque masks.

The 370 costumes used last night are said to have cost nearly $600,000. The Teatro dell'Opera expects to sell them, along with the stage sets, to the Royal Opera House at Covent Garden in London after a Rome run of seven performances.

Later this winter and spring the Rome Opera promises to offer Mozart's *Così Fan Tutte* (in a Covent Garden production), Verdi's *Macbeth,* Rimsky-Korsakov's *Le Coq d'Or,* Donizetti's *L'Elisir d'Amore,* Puccini's *Madama Butterfly,* and the ballet *Romeo and Juliet* to Tchaikovsky's music. Alas, the future is never certain for the Teatro dell'Opera.

The new manager, Vidusso, resigned on the eve of yesterday's gala, explaining he was disgusted with the "blackmail" that the employees of the institution had been attempting.

• Foul Air •

JANUARY 19

Private car traffic was prohibited throughout the city from three to nine P.M. today because air pollution had reached the danger level during the last few days. The chronic smog in Rome is caused almost exclusively by engine exhausts; there is very little smokestack industry in and around the Italian capital, and most of the heating is now done with natural gas, which is relatively clean.

If you ride in a bus or in the subway you hear coughing and sneezing all the time, and you may catch a running nose or sore throat yourself. The soiled atmosphere has led to a rash of respiratory ailments, health officials, pharmacists, and hospitals say. Pollution emergencies occur every time Rome remains without winds for a few days, which fortunately doesn't happen often. The *tempestates* gods sweep our sky most of the time.

This week so far has been colder than most people here like, but windless; the traffic is spasmodic again after a comparative lull during Rome's long yuletide season. Yesterday the nine air quality monitoring posts around the city reported an alarming increase in carbon monoxide.

The six-hour ban on cars today won't help much; rather than providing actual relief, it was a symbolic gesture meant to get Romans used to public transport, which isn't, alas, very efficient. The no-driving time span was too short, and there were too many exceptions. Official and police vehicles, taxis, cars of physically disadvantaged persons, and all automobiles with catalytic converters were allowed to circulate. Equally, Rome's hundreds of thousands of motorcycles and motor scooters had free rein and swarmed out like excited bees.

Furthermore, quite a few Romans seemed to be flouting City Hall's antismog edict, using their cars in the hope that they wouldn't be caught at one of the few roadblocks or by municipal police patrols. Some who were apprehended said they didn't read the newspapers or hadn't heard of the ban from broadcasts; they were fined all the same. But it wouldn't be Rome if one couldn't somehow procure fake windshield badges attesting that one is handicapped or that one's car has catalytic equipment. The cops waved on vehicles so marked; I saw no one making a spot check.

• Another Plaque •

JANUARY 20

The mayor put on the green, white, and red sash of his office and had himself driven to the Via Veneto to unveil a plaque commemorating Federico Fellini. The filmmaker would have been seventy-five years old today (he died in Rome in 1993). His sister and the sister of his late widow, the actress Giulietta Masina, were present at the little ceremony.

Thus Fellini joined the Roman emperors and consuls, saints and popes, artists like Michelangelo, composers, national heroes, and an American astronaut, whose names are all engraved on the stones of this city.

The white tablet at the corner of Via Veneto and Via Ludovisi proclaims that the movie director "made of the Via Veneto the theater of the Dolce Vita." The upper stretch of the rising, curving boulevard indeed provided the setting for key scenes of the celebrated picture; Fellini himself, however, often said that the sweet life was largely imaginary, and that *his* Via Veneto was the plywood and plaster set built for him in Theater No. 5 of the Cinecittà studios.

Somebody should count and catalog all the lapidary memorials in Rome. There must be hundreds of them, not considering the hieroglyphs with the names of pharaohs and lists of their victories on the dozen Egyptian obelisks in various spots around the city, nor the proud testimonials by Marcus Vipsanius Agrippa, the son-in-law and general of Emperor Augustus, on the architrave of the Pantheon, and by Pope Paul V on the front frieze of St. Peter's, nor finally all those dedications and fulsome tributes on a plethora of other buildings and monuments.

I have long spotted marble memorials of Ariosto, Goethe, Keats, Shelly, Joyce, Mascagni, and many others.

After many years of living in Rome I still run into some marble, travertine, or bronze memento that I haven't noticed before. Only the other day I deciphered a darkened plaque at 18 Piazza Barberini that I must have seen hundreds of times without taking the trouble to read. The almost illegible text records that Bjørnstjerne Bjørnson, the Norwegian poet and writer who in 1903 received the Nobel Prize for literature, once stayed there.

Some of the countless inscriptions in this city are in languages other than Latin or Italian. A stone with a bust and a laurel wreath, in bronze, at 125 Via Sistina recalls in Russian that Nikolai Vasilievich Gogol lived and worked there, 1838–42. An Italian translation on the same stone skips the patronymic, identifying the author of the *Dead Souls* as Nicola Gogol. No mention is made of the Antico Caffè Greco down the Spanish Stairs where Gogol did much of his writing.

A tablet on a medieval building at 96 Piazza Farnese records in Swedish that Saint Bridget stayed in that nunnery for nineteen years until her death in 1373. A square plaque on the United States Consulate, 121 Via Veneto, states in English that on June 4, 1944, when Allied forces liberated Rome from Nazi occupation, Brigadier General Robert F. Frederick, commander of the United States–Canadian First Special Services Force, established his headquarters in the building. The adjacent United States Embassy, a sumptuous 110-year-old palazzo, is described by a large marble plaque in Italian as a "royal residence" in which the dowager Queen Margherita lived for twenty-six years as the widow of King Umberto I (her cousin), who was assassinated in 1900.

The astronaut who was honored by a Roman plaque is Michael Collins. His name is on the facade of the house, 16 Corso d'Italia, where he was born in 1930. The Italian inscription praises him as "intrepid" and declares that Rome "is proud of this son of hers." Collins was the third member of the *Apollo 11* mission, together with Neil A. Armstrong and Edwin E. Aldrich, Jr.

With such a multitude of tributes committed to stone, I have always been puzzled by Rome's failure to commemorate some of the greats of history or the arts who were its guests—maybe I have just never come across their plaques. I have never seen, for instance, an open-air inscription referring to Raphael here, excepting the business sign of the Raphael Hotel, although there is of course the artful Latin epitaph composed by his humanist friend Cardinal Bembo on the painter's tomb in the Pantheon. In Alexander Pope's twisted rendering: "Living, great Nature feared he might outvie her works; and dying, fears herself may die." The building near the Vatican that Raphael bought from Bramante in 1517, and where he lived, worked, and died, has long been razed.

Mozart has long lacked his Rome tablet. He visited the city with his father as a fourteen-year-old in 1770, and the pope awarded the Order of the Golden Spur to the sensationally gifted lad. About three hundred years later City Hall caught up with his fame: on the city's far eastern outskirts there is now a Via W. A. Mozart; it is near the Largo Bach, the Via Schubert, the Piazza Brahms, and the Via Bartók, all marked with Rome's travertine street signs.

As for the Via Veneto, there is still plenty of room for commemorative plaques on the facades of its stately buildings because the famous street—meant as Rome's answer to the Avenue des Champs-Elysées in Paris—is relatively young. When the Excelsior Hotel, a key prop in the Fellini film, was opened in 1906, much of the area around it was still taken up by gardens and vineyards. The serpentine boulevard was laid out just before World War I and eventually received the name of the Alpine town, Vittorio Veneto, where the Italian army, beefed up with Allied units, decisively defeated the Austro-Hungarian forces in 1918. If you ask Romans today for directions to Via Vittorio Veneto, they will blink and eventually say, "You mean Via Veneto?"

• Mammoth Monument •

After dark I see from my windows a new, luminous point of reference, a couple of miles distant, in the immense panorama of the city below. The mayor has in fact decided to have the huge, garishly white monument to Victor Emmanuel II, the Vittoriano, floodlighted at night. The two bronze quadrigas at its top have incongruously been fitted with powerful spotlights like twin beacons, and it seems they direct their beams toward us.

The Defense Ministry, in a concerted move, has ordered the reopening of the interior halls of the eighty-year-old marble leviathan at the north side of Capitol Hill, which have long been inaccessible to the public. Does all this portend a reawakening of nationalism?

The military establishment wields jurisdiction over the monument because it is also the site of Italy's Tomb of the Unknown Soldier. Flames flicker from twin bronze torches at either side of the tomb; an honor guard flanks it; the president of the republic ceremonially pays tribute to it; and foreign dignitaries on official visits lay wreaths there.

The cavernous interior of the giant marble structure holds the Museum of the Risorgimento, that nineteenth-century political movement and the resulting wars whereby Italy—with substantial help from France and Prussia—achieved national unity. Risorgimento memorabilia, as well as tattered regimental banners and old uniforms from the nineteenth century and from World War I, are treasured inside the monument.

An equestrian statue of King Victor Emmanuel II (1820–87), the coarse-grained, soldierly ruler of Sardinia-Piedmont and eventually of unified Italy, towers above the marble sepulcher containing the bones of an anonymous infantryman plucked from a World War I battlefield.

When I walked down the Via Nazionale on the first evening of my first visit to Rome, I was stunned by a row of brightly illuminated tall white columns that I saw through a side street. I thought I was glimpsing the majestic remains of an ancient temple. Descending into the Piazza Venezia, I realized that the columns belonged to a modern white marble pile cluttered with sculptures, reliefs, gold decorations, and fountains. It was floodlighted then as it is again now.

Mussolini's dictatorship glorified the monument, which it called the "Altar of the Fatherland." Il Duce had his headquarters in the somber Renaissance building diagonally across the Piazza Venezia, and he often mounted the steps to the Tomb of the Unknown Soldier in Fascist ceremonies or in connection with military parades.

Since World War II when all of Rome was blacked out at night, the Vittoriano has rarely been illuminated. Crossing the Piazza Venezia after dark one could see the eternal flames marking the Tomb of the Unknown Soldier, a symbol much more eloquent than all the marble, bronze, and gold bombast around it.

The Vittoriano, a prime example of architectural rhetoric, won admiration from the German Emperor Wilhelm II and appealed to Fascist chauvinism. It was designed by Count Giuseppe Sacconi and chosen from among more than three hundred entries in a competition; his original project called for even more florid ornamentation than it would eventually display. Work began in 1885. Sacconi slipped into insanity, maybe because of his frustration over the slowness of construction progress, and he died in 1905. The memorial, to which many artists contributed over the years, swallowed a sizable portion of the taxes paid by an entire genera-tion of Italians. Unveiled in 1911, it was completed only in 1927.

The glaring white marble that so impressed me when I first saw it at night will, by its mineralogical nature, never mellow; it can-not get the soft patina of the Colosseum and other ancient struc-tures built with the porous travertine that is Rome's own stone. The marble blocks for the Vittoriano came from Brescia in Italy's north, apparently at the insistence of Giuseppe Zanardelli, an influential politician who eventually became prime minister; he wanted to favor his home province.

By its location near the center of Rome, at the southern end of the straight Via del Corso, the Victor Emmanuel Monument oblit-erated the view of the Capitol Hill's northern slope; it also domi-nates the city's panorama from many angles. Tourists have long called the marble monstrosity the Wedding Cake, a sugary con-fection 443 feet wide and 230 feet tall. Another frequent compar-ison views the Vittoriano as a giant, old-style typewriter. The Florentine writer Giovanni Papini called the monument after its official inauguration in 1911 a deluxe urinal.

Seventy-five years later a local bank that often sponsors con-servation projects launched a "Trial of the Vittoriano." Some archi-tects, artists, and urbanists publicly advocated its demolition. Other experts who offered testimony to the mock court admitted that the monument was hideous, but they defended its continued existence on the ground that it represented a period of national history. Rome's current mayor, who heads a left-wing administra-tion, declared that the Vittoriano, a neighbor to City Hall, was "absolutely undervalued" and might become a "great museum of war and peace."

February

• Fashion Fizzle •

FEBRUARY 1

The spring and summer showings by local fashion designers that
ended today seemed more a requiem for what was meant to be
Roman haute couture than a triumph. The grand finale brought
out the police.

Valentino and the few other internationally known ateliers still
based in the Italian capital have long shifted the semiannual
parades of their collections to Paris or Milan. Fashion writers and
professional buyers from the United States, Japan, and Germany
again stayed away from the Rome event. The only one of the
world's supermodels who cared to stalk down a Rome catwalk was

an Italian, Carla Bruni; after a few lucrative hours here she was again on a Paris-bound flight.

Rome's dream of becoming a global center of high fashion was a byproduct of "Hollywood on the Tiber" during the giddy late 1950s and early 1960s when American-Italian coproductions were made in the Cinecittà studios and on locations all around the city. Former family seamstresses suddenly found themselves draping fabrics around the shoulders of the likes of Ava Gardner, Elizabeth Taylor, and Audrey Hepburn. One of those veterans of the needle, Micol Fontana, was a showroom guest when the latest cycle of presentations opened on the Capitol the day before yesterday.

Long after the dolce vita euphoria had ended with a hangover of disillusionment and debt, Rome bravely continued seeking recognition as an international style capital; twice a year a haute couture week was held here, promoted by the Chamber of Commerce. Diminishing returns led to the first defections. Now the periodic fashion circus has shrunk to a three-day affair of hardly more than local importance, and today there was talk of further whittling it down to one day.

With ill-concealed glee, *Corriere della Sera* of Milan, Italy's most important newspaper, proclaimed in a headline the "agony" of Roman high fashion. Milan, of course, keeps going strong in the ready-to-wear sector while also nurturing haute couture ambitions.

Valentino and the few other important Roman couturiers now hold their presentations in Paris or Milan because there is no such market here for exclusive, pricy dresses as there is in Paris, New York, or even Milan. Designers here say starlets, media beauties, and wives and mistresses of the rich and powerful (in whom the capital abounds) want to borrow their creations or get them for free rather than buy them.

The style-conscious cross section of Roman society that attended the showings of the last three days probably didn't include many prospective customers. Only the lines of high-class wedding dresses that were displayed may actually be sold here; Rome loves lavish marriages. The audiences were made up mainly of mature socialites who wouldn't miss any smart party; show-business personalities hankering for publicity; and some genuine or fake aristocrats. A red-haired woman whom press agents billed as a relative of Prince Rainier of Monaco was quickly discovered to be a social climber from Sicily.

To me, a fashion illiterate, the setting of the shows were more captivating than the styles. The mayor made a hall near his office available for the more important presentations. Milan, Paris, or New York can't match the panorama from his Senatorial Palace on the Capitol: an incomparable view of the Roman Forum spreads below, an ironically permanent backdrop for fashions that should last only a season.

For the minor collections, including one by graduates of the local fashion academy, the city offered the restored former Roman Aquarium, a free-standing structure built before World War I near the main railroad terminal. When I first visited Rome, the curious building no longer contained any fish, and even the water tanks had been ripped out; it was then used to house an ancient statuary that had been dug up in or around the city and awaited placement in a museum or collection. I had gone to the Piazza Manfredo Fanti, where the aquarium rises, not to view sea monsters but to inspect one of the few surviving stretches of the tufa walls that encircled republican Rome.

According to tradition, those walls were built by Servius Tullius, the semilegendary sixth king of Rome, but scholars say that the republican officials of the fourth century B.C. had it erected, probably by Greek contractors, to protect the city from another such invasion as that by the Gauls in 390 B.C.

During the last several years the Piazza Manfredo Fanti (named after a nineteenth-century general) and the turn-of-the-century buildings around it looked increasingly seedy. City Hall's decision to have the aquarium restored and used for exhibitions and events like the fashion shows is part of an attempt to rehabilitate the poky neighborhood.

Some local firms that wanted to take part in the Rome fashion affair but weren't admitted to the Capitol spurned the aquarium and instead rented halls in the Grand and Plaza Hotels. As usual there was a lot of bad-mouthing and backbiting among rival designers, which found its way into the gossip press. As an inelegant coda to the couture medley an uproar occurred at the Senatorial Palace this afternoon.

Prince Egon von Fürstenberg, an aging playboy who set himself up as a stylist some years ago, managed to show his collection on the Capitol. He sent out more than six hundred invitations to his many friends among the rich and glamourous, although the hall has seats for only 280. It seems that almost every invitee showed up, in addition to the inevitable contingent of gate-crashers. When the hall was filled to capacity the doors were closed and people outside started pummeling them, fighting among themselves, and clashing with police officers who had rushed to the scene.

A shirt-sleeved Prince Fürstenberg plowed into the irate crowd to rescue a few prospective customers. Shouting and shoving in the corridors of the Senatorial Palace continued through the entire show, and the mayor (who wasn't present) defensively stated later that he had only lent the premises. He had nothing to do with organizing the fashion events.

Whether he wants it or not, Fürstenberg will get plenty of publicity thanks to the paparazzi who were out in force. The prince personifies a blend of Swabian-descended German nobility and Italian money. He is a nephew of Gianni Agnelli, the president of the giant Fiat motor company. A bevy of Agnelli heiresses was in the audience to look at the Fürstenberg collection—the prince's mother with her second husband, an aunt, and a cousin. Another aunt is Italy's present foreign minister, but she wasn't there. I wonder whether the Agnelli women actually wear Fürstenberg creations.

• Stranglers •

FEBRUARY 6

The police today announced criminal usury charges against two elderly Romans, a man and a woman, both of them ostensibly on welfare. The two, said to have been loan-sharking independently of each other, were found to have habitual use of chauffeured limousines, to have big bank accounts, and to have caches of gold and other valuables in their homes. The couple have apartments in different buildings near the main railroad terminal, both curiously owned by the same landlord, who was identified by his mob nickname, Enzuccio. According to the police, Enzuccio is suspected to be the courier of a drug gang and, if needed, would collect payments due to the two loan sharks from tardy debtors.

The chief of the police squad on the case said that a few months ago the owner of a mechanical workshop had borrowed the equivalent of $12,500 from the male welfare client and had been told a few days ago he now owed $25,000. Such exorbitant debt growth is by no means unusual in the local loan-sharking pond, where the going interest rates at present are 20 to 25 percent *monthly.* The police spokesman stated it took some persuasion to induce the hapless witness to lodge a formal complaint against his creditor. He had already received the kind of threats that are routine enforcement tactics in the racket.

State television in its main news broadcast last night showed a man with his back to the camera who described himself as a merchant entangled in a loan-sharking ring; when he once failed to come up with an interest installment, he said, a debt collector amiably remarked: "That's your boy, that nice blond kid I see going to school every morning?" The sinister implication was that gangsters would hurt or kidnap the child if his father didn't pay.

The affair of these two limousine-riding welfare recipients has once again focused public attention on widespread usury in Rome; it has existed since antiquity but has become more rampant since the influx of drug money seeking investment opportunities has combined with the know-how and muscle of the mafia. The loan-sharking boom is fostered by the inefficiency and bureaucratic methods of the local banks.

The owner of a small auto repair shop near where I live told me the other day: "I have been to all the bank branches around here, and none will lend me money when I can't pay the salaries of my three workers. I know I can repay quickly because my shop is full of cars to fix, and their owners won't get them back before they settle their bills. What can I do? I go to the *cravattero* to get the cash I need for a few days."

Cravattero translates as "necktie man," and in the current Roman slang has the same meaning as the much older *strozzino* (strangler); both terms, implying suffocation, stand for loan shark. Apparently a lot of people know their local strangler, who is often camouflaged as the manager of some legitimate business like a fruit stand at an outdoor market, a real estate agency, or an appliance store. In fact, a middle-aged woman I know who works as a secretary in a lawyer's office is rumored to be lending money at high interest on the side. The wife of a municipal employee, she used to administer the funds of the condominium—close to our building—where she and her husband live, but the board soon suspected her of dipping into the funds for her credit operations and took her responsibilities away.

The shylocking plague has become so virulent that the Rome merchants' confederation a few weeks ago had a special toll-free number, 855-1111, set up for anonymous complaints by victims. It may have been such a tipoff that led to the raid on the office and home of a high-living tax consultant about whom I have heard a lot in the past. I don't know him personally, but I know his girlfriend. She told me that at the ungodly hour of five one recent morning no fewer than a dozen Carabinieri appeared with a search warrant and systematically combed the premises, seizing all the files and computer disks. "I moved out the same day," the young woman confided.

According to the merchants' confederation, one in every five small- and medium-sized businesses here—stores, artisans' workshops, travel agencies, espresso bars, restaurants, and nightclubs above all—is in the clutches of racketeers. At times there will be arson, a bombing, a car theft, some other sabotage, or even murder to extort money or punish nonpayment, but what the loan sharks really want, the merchants' organization asserts, is to take over legitimate firms. For instance, a beauty parlor or a pizzeria that has turned to a strangler for credit may soon be owned in part, and eventually wholly, by mafiosi who use it for laundering drug money. A high-ranking police officer, Alessandro Pansa, declared yesterday: "Organized crime is seeking a legal umbrella to recycle huge amounts of cash."

The newspapers ominously suggest that Rome's Magliana gang is deeply involved in loan-sharking. Earlier, police sources claimed the near-mythical crime syndicate had been completely stamped out. Maybe it wasn't, after all.

• Dark Workshops •

FEBRUARY 10

The Democratic Party of the Left, as the former, formidable Italian Communist Party now calls itself, let it be known today it is selling its national headquarters building at the center of Rome. Still a major political force, the P.D.S.—the initials of its Italian name—is burdened with considerably more than $200 million in pressing debts; it has already sold various properties here and in provincial cities.

The massive edifice at 4 Via della Botteghe Oscure has a brownish red facade on the upper stories over the yellow-gray travertine facing of the two lower floors. Known as the "red palace," it has been the symbol and power center of the mightiest Marxist machine outside the Soviet orbit for nearly half a century. I have never succeeded in getting into it above the street floor. As a reporter for an American newspaper I was at most admitted to a bare press room near the main entrance, which was guarded day and night by police and the party's own stalwarts.

I was always reminded of a layperson's visit to a monastery: if they let you in at all, you will find yourself in an inhospitable parlor outside the cloistered part of the building. There were other parallels between the Communist Party and the Roman Catholic Church—their theology, their hierarchies, the devotion and discipline of their militants. I found it curious that Communist headquarters was only a stone's throw from the Church of the Gesù in which Saint Ignatius of Loyola, the founder of the Jesuit Order, is buried. The Communist apparatchiks whom I used to meet from time to time—not at party headquarters but over lunch in some distant trattoria—might as well have been Jesuits; they were well educated, often witty, pragmatic, and reticent.

The address of the red palace has a somewhat ominous ring: *Via delle Botteghe Oscure* means street of the dark workshops. It seems that the neighborhood was once honeycombed with the cavernous workplaces of artisans; there is also a story of prostitutes having plied their trade there. Members of the Communist apparatus used to call the headquarters building *il bottegone*, the big shop.

The stately seven-story structure went up during World War II and was supposed to house a bank. It was, instead, acquired by the Communist Party soon after the end of the war and readapted for its own purposes. There was much speculation as to where the money for the purchase had come from. One stubborn rumor holds that its origin was gold and other valuables that Communist partisans had found on Mussolini when they captured him on Lake Como as he was trying to flee to Switzerland with his mistress, Claretta Petacci, in April 1945. According to a different version it was Moscow that had subsidized the real estate investment in Rome. There is plenty of evidence that the Italian Communist Party received direct and indirect financial aid from the Soviet Union until the late 1980s. When Communists were recently confronted with this fact they didn't make much of an effort to deny it, but they contended that some Soviet assistance might have been reasonable because the United States had for decades been bankrolling anti-Communist groups in Italy. The end of the Cold War, at any rate, dried up such underground funding, and one consequence is that the Via delle Botteghe Oscure building is now up for sale.

Unfortunately, for the Democratic Party of the Left, the real estate market in Rome is soft at the moment. The P.D.S. would like to get something around $35 million for its national headquarters with its nearly 65,000 square feet of office space in a prime downtown location. However, it seems doubtful that such an amount can be obtained unless the party finds a foreign investor paying in hard currency. Offers from some multinational corporation planning to establish a highly representative Italian branch, or from an international hotel chain wanting to open a new unit in Rome, maybe in view of the Holy Year 2000, would be welcome.

The forbidding Communist headquarters served as an unlikely love nest in 1947. Palmiro Togliatti, then the powerful national secretary of the Italian Communist Party and a ranking international Communist leader, lived there for six months in a prosaically furnished suite on the seventh floor with his mistress, Leonilde (Nilde) Iotti. Togliatti, a veteran of the international Marxist-Leninist movement who had served as a political commissar in the Spanish Civil War, spent the World War II years in the notorious Hotel Lux in Moscow with his wife, Rita Montagnana, also a longtime Communist militant. Back in Italy at the end of the war after many years abroad, Togliatti, who hailed from northern Italy, succumbed to the Roman atmosphere in more than one way.

He became minister of justice for a short period, and an influential member of Parliament for the rest of his life. In the Chamber of Deputies he met a young Communist legislator, Nilde, and started a much-noticed liaison with her. Those were the years of the incipient dolce vita, but the dour functionaries of the Communist apparatus were shocked. When Togliatti openly split up with his wife, who was admired throughout the party, and wanted to set up house with his new girlfriend, the prudish Communist leadership obliged him to do so in secret—in two dull rooms on the top floor of the red palace.

Only after a while did the couple manage to move into a place of their own on the northeastern outskirts of Rome and go through a marriage ceremony in the Soviet Union, which under Italian law was invalid. If the building on the Via delle Botteghe

Oscure ever becomes a hotel, the seventh-floor Togliatti-Iotti rooms should become the bridal suite.

It must have been at the time of the idyll at Communist headquarters that I ran into the couple during a Sunday outing in the Roman hillside. I don't exactly remember the year, but I could still find the spot of that encounter. It was on the footpath leading to the summit of the Monte Cavo, the highest elevation of the Alban Hills, at a point where it runs close to the ancient Roman road, paved with flagstones, that rises to what in antiquity was a shrine of Jupiter.

I was then climbing the footpath across a forest of old chestnut and oak trees more quickly than I would now, and was about to overtake a middle-aged man and a chubby young woman. They were walking slowly and were unmistakably having a tiff, raising their voices. In a show of discretion I made a little detour on the slope and hurriedly got above them. Glancing sidewise, however, I recognized them at once. I had seen them often from the press gallery of the Chamber of Deputies, and had repeatedly fired questions at Togliatti together with the usual crowd of Italian reporters when we had the chance to approach him. He couldn't have remembered me—if he looked at me at all—on the path up the Monte Cavo, absorbed as he appeared in quarreling with his girlfriend, and I gave no sign of knowing who they were. Maybe Nilde was pressing the Communist leader to get them a real home that wasn't under constant surveillance by the party apparatus.

What is the national leadership of the P.D.S. going to do when it relinquishes the *bottegone,* the red palace on the Via delle Botteghe Oscure? It may rent or buy other, more modest premises in some convenient location in Rome—I have heard of a building in the Esquilino Section near the Colosseum—or it may take over one of the party's existing branch offices around town. The Rome telephone directory still lists eighty P.D.S. sections, or neighborhood units, each with its own office and telephone number—almost as many as there are Roman Catholic parishes in the city of the popes.

The former Communist Party is still the strongest and best-organized political force in the Italian capital, although it was repudiated by quite a few hard-liners when it changed its name and abandoned Marxist orthodoxy after the collapse of the Soviet Union. The old-timers set up a new splinter group, the Party of Communist Reconstruction, and are clinging to the hammer-and-sickle emblem.

The Democratic Party of the Left, instead, adopted a new symbol, an oak; hammer and sickle remain still visible in a small medallion on the tree trunk, but it may soon disappear. Whenever I see that oak I think of the trees on the slope of Monte Cavo.

• Kiddie Carnival •

FEBRUARY 23

This is the last day of Carnival, tomorrow is Ash Wednesday. Post offices, law courts, and government departments closed for the day at noon and many stores at one P.M. so that their staffs could celebrate. Yet the only Roman Carnival living up to its old reputation took place at the Teatro dell'Opera last month during the first act of Berlioz's *Benvenuto Cellini* when the chorus sang *"Venez, venez, peuple de Rome!"* and fantastic masks invaded the stage.

The masks I saw today were worn by children dressed up as Fairy Queens, Snow Whites, or Robin Hoods who were being led by adults to various parties at homes around the city. All January and February the sidewalks were covered with confetti that youngsters had showered on passersby. A more recent, and nastier, carnival custom here is spraying other people with shaving cream, whether you know them or not. Savvy Romans put on old clothes today if they had to go out. It was an unseasonably warm day, and fur coats, a favorite target of sprayers, were rare.

Little girls wearing hoopskirts and conical fairy-tale hats looked ten years older with their face powder, eye shadow, lipstick, and beauty spots—a local carnival makeup job that always saddens me. Isn't there time for that; why not let seven-year-olds just be children? Why make them into Lolitas at carnival time?

Tonight some grown-ups too went to parties, dances held in private or in a few restaurants and night spots that had advertised special carnival affairs. All this of course was a far cry from the carnival merrymaking when Goethe or Stendhal were guests of the city. Coaches filled with Roman aristocrats, rich people, and courtesans in their best finery and attended by liveried grooms, would drive up and down the narrow Corso in an unending procession between the crowds of the curious on the sidelines amid showers of confetti.

I am told that actual carnival parades with floats, masked marchers, and musical bands were held in a few suburbs and in nearby towns last Thursday and today, but even the local television channels ignored them—carnival footage from Rio de Janeiro, Nice, Venice, or Cologne was better. "Roman Carnival" is no longer anything but a phrase.

The only people who indulged in exceptional public revelry today were a couple of hundred German soccer fans who had come to Rome for a European Cup match between the Borussia team of Dortmund and the local Lazio club. Wearing the Borussia's colors, yellow and black, the Germans took over the square in front of the Trevi Fountain and the Spanish Stairs this afternoon, cheering their club, taking pictures of one another, and drinking several crates of Dortmund beer they had brought with them. A few dozen Lazio supporters gathered in the Spanish Square and heckled the guests, but it was all rather good-natured. I later found out that the Lazio trounced the visiting Dortmunders in an evening game.

• Third-World Parade •

FEBRUARY 25

Recent immigrants from other continents, maybe as many as forty thousand, paraded across the center of Rome this afternoon to demonstrate against racial discrimination and violence. At the tail end of a listless carnival period and amidst general worries about the plunging lira and rising taxes, the capital thus was forced to give thought to a bundle of problems that many Romans just want to go away.

It was something of a first in the city's long history. Sure enough, Germanic and Illyric legions marched in Rome in the declining Roman Empire; the city was looted by barbarian and Saracen invaders during the Middle Ages and by rampaging mercenaries during the Sack of Rome, A.D. 1527; French troops marched in the city at various times; Hitler's retreating panzer divisions passed through the Italian capital in 1944; and the conquering Allied forces occupied it. Yet never before has the city seen such a vast, peaceful march of nonwhites.

I watched them surge into the Piazza del Popolo where their parade ended, and a couple of hours were filled with speeches, songs, and dancing. The mood was outwardly joyous rather than angry or truculent, although the marchers had plenty to complain about. Many ugly racial incidents have occurred during the last several weeks; a few days ago young white punks closed in on a visibly pregnant Somali woman in the seaside district of Ostia, punching and kicking her.

There were Africans and Asians from all over Italy in the Piazza del Popolo—Tunisians, Algerians, Moroccans, Nigerians, the tall Senegalese sidewalk vendors, East Africans, Pakistanis, and Bangladeshis. A group of blacks carried a sign identifying them as metalworkers from northern Italy, evidence that at least a few of the newcomers had found industrial jobs.

Many thousands of the marchers had been brought to Rome from various parts of the nation in four special railroad trains and a hundred chartered buses. The demonstration was organized by labor unions and by local volunteer groups, most of which are led by Roman Catholic human rights activists. Among the few white Italians in the rally was the bishop of Caserta, Raffaele Nogaro, who has long championed the interests of the thousands of non-white laborers who pluck tomatoes and do other farmwork in the fertile plains near Naples.

I walked close to the bishop and heard him say into a reporter's microphone that it was absurd on the part of the Italian authorities to issue residence permits to immigrants only if they had work contracts, when one legally gets a job in Italy solely if one has a residence permit. This is the catch-22 for foreigners here. One of the many streamers I saw in the square read WE ARE ALL CLANDES-TINES.

Clandestini is how the information media usually describe the foreigners who are in Italy without residence permits and who somehow make a living here. Officially they are 400,000—in addition to 600,000 recent immigrants living legally in Italy—but their actual number is probably much higher. There is little concealment about the existence of the so-called clandestine residents: many of them wash the dishes in restaurant kitchens, bake pizzas in full sight of the patrons, harvest artichokes in the fields, sell sunglasses on the beaches and cheap umbrellas in subway stations when it rains, and push the baby carriages of middle-class families or the wheelchairs of invalids. Their own children go to Italian schools. Some of the recent immigrants—whites from eastern Europe among them—engage in prostitution, and some in crime.

Nobody knows exactly how many legal and "clandestine" immigrants live in Rome at present; they may well be far more than 200,000—one in every twelve or fifteen residents. Whether old-timers are aware of it or not (many don't want to see), the hundreds of thousands of foreigners who have joined Rome's population during the last few decades form a new underclass that has profoundly changed the city's flavor. Non-Italian people are conspicuous, sometimes even dominant, in every subway car or bus. Many will stay on in the city and have children who will speak the *romanesco* dialect and, it is hoped, rise in life.

It's nothing new. Nineteen hundred years ago Juvenal railed at Rome's having become a "city of Greeks." Teachers of grammar and rhetoric, geometers, painters, masseurs, prophets, tightrope walkers, physicians, wizards, and prostitutes all were Greeks or Syrians, "blown to Rome by the wind," the satirist—who himself had come from the southern provinces of Italy—complained in hexameters. Many of the immigrants then had skills that the Romans lacked, and they didn't organize any protest marches.

In the Piazza del Popolo today I didn't see any of the thousands of Filipino maids and nannies who work for Roman families. Nor were there any of the eastern Europeans who have drifted to Rome since the late 1980s. Many of them are educated people who don't care to mix with unskilled immigrants. There are also class distinctions in the underclass.

I had a vivid impression of the changes in the Roman street scene that the influx of poor foreigners has produced when, the night before yesterday, I met a visitor at the railroad terminal and took her in a cab to the apartment of mutual friends in the

Trastevere district where she was to stay. We were both struck by the proliferation of windshield washers at the major intersections. We saw at least fifty of them during our ten-minute trip, counting half a dozen alone on the Garibaldi Bridge.

The platoon on the bridge ignored our taxi, well knowing that not even a fifty-lire coin is to be got out of a cabbie, but they missed none of the other cars that were waiting for the traffic light on the Trastevere side to change. They wiped windshields more or less thoroughly even though the drivers behind them might make the Roman gesture for "nothing doing"—the spread thumb and forefinger slowly shaken from side to side. I noticed one motorist slipping a 1,000-lire bill to a youngster who was spraying the windshield with detergent (or plain water) from a can. Worth about 60¢ at the current exchange rate, 1,000 lire seems to be the present top fee, if you pay at all.

Virtually all the people wielding rags and brushes at the intersections we passed were nonwhite. Only a few years ago when this way of asking for a handout suddenly became common here, it was always a blond, young fellow, sometimes wearing eyeglasses, who approached one's car, politely greeted, and proceeded to wash the windshield, although it may have undergone similar treatment one intersection earlier. The blond men with their neat plastic buckets were Poles—refugees or émigrés.

The Polish monopoly of windshield washing in Rome didn't last long. The original practitioners either found better things to do here or, more likely, moved on to other western countries. Newcomers from Africa and Asia have taken over the niche that the Poles abandoned and are now crowding it. Shadowy gangs are controlling intersections with heavy traffic, assigning windshield-cleaning slots and roughing up outsiders who try to squeeze in. A mob concession on the Garibaldi Bridge, with kickbacks paid to the area boss, may mean social advancement of sorts to an undocumented immigrant who for months has been slaving on some farm, only to be told by the owner, as it happens sometimes, "I can't pay you because I haven't been paid by the dealer who bought my eggplants."

While the windshield washers are busy at the intersections, hundreds of Senegalese who somehow made it to Rome spread their merchandise on the sidewalks of the Via Ottaviano near the Vatican and other busy streets as well as in subway stations— leather belts, handbags, African-style headwear with gold embroidery, Taiwan-made copper articles, and fake Louis Vuitton products are among their wares. Sometimes the municipal police tolerate the illegal trade, sometimes they go through the motions of clamping down. The Senegalese hastily stuff their wares into huge black canvas bags and slink off. In Rome, the West African street merchants don't have—not yet, maybe—the sleek attaché cases in which their colleagues in New York peddle their faux Swiss watches.

I know no Roman family that still has native Italian household help. Some maids are Eritreans or Somalis who already spoke a little Italian when they came to Rome from their countries, which were once Italian colonies. As for the Filipinas, most of them arrived with regular work permits, procured by Roman Catholic organizations and nuns' orders. In my neighborhood I hear Filipino maids chat in Tagalog with one another; the elderly contessa who lives in her villa nearby employs a Filipino butler-gardener. To have a Filipina maid, nanny, or nurse is classy and isn't cheap. Some of them earned academic degrees at home but couldn't find any of the jobs for which they are qualified, and most Filipinas send money to the families they left behind.

When they step off the airplane from Manila, they already know the going minimum hourly rate for household work in Rome, and through the Filipino network here they quickly learn of the benefits to which they are entitled under Italy's benevolent social legislation. Lately, women from Poland and other eastern European countries have begun vying with the well-liked Filipinas for household work.

Tides of immigrants from underdeveloped countries and from Europe's east have rolled also into the other of the affluent western European nations; the battalions of foreign prostitutes who have invaded Italy and especially Rome during the last few years seem nevertheless exceptional. I don't know the reasons; maybe it's easier to get into Italy than into France, Switzerland, or Germany— or is the Italian market more promising? The newcomers to the old flesh trade here have long swept the native practitioners off the streets and into call girl networks.

Italian newsmagazines that cater to pruriency through pseudo-sociological inquiries and soft-core artwork periodically publish detailed maps of Roman whoredom, presumably as a service for their male readers. They are thus informed that Nigerians and Ghanaians hustle in the EUR (World's Fair) district and on the Viale Togliatti on the eastern outskirts, the young women from eastern Europe who seem to be much in demand work the Via Veneto near the luxury hotels and around the central railroad terminal, the Latin American transvestites pick up customers in the Villa Borghese gardens, and so forth.

In our cab ride the other night we saw a couple of pretty blond streetwalkers who may have come recently from the Czech Republic patrolling an area at the center that to my knowledge wasn't frequented by prostitutes until recently. The field seems expanding and increasingly crowded. The press routinely reports stabbings, slashings, and even murders in turf wars involving prostitutes and pimps.

Prostitution in itself isn't punishable in Italy today, but soliciting in public places and exploitation of prostitution are. To get the whoremongering off the streets and out of parked cars, every now and then some columnist or maverick legislator suggests repeal of the 1958 law that closed the licensed bordellos. It seems highly unlikely, though, that they will be reopened—certainly not before the Church's Holy Year 2000 is over.

March

• New Olympics? •

<u>MARCH 2</u>

In addition to the looming Holy Year 2000, does Rome need another mega-event a few years later? Mayor Francesco Rutelli thinks so, and in his office on the Capitol today he launched what he described as his Olympic Project. It calls for a "pre-feasibility study" with a view to later announcing the city's bid for hosting the Summer Olympic Games in 2004, forty-four years after the global event was first held here. The mayor suggested that if Rome loses out to South Africa, Beijing, Istanbul, or some other candidate for 2004, it might reapply to the International Olympic Committee for 2008.

Most Romans appear convinced that the youthful, personable mayor is thinking of a second term after his present one ends in 1997; today's move will inevitably be interpreted as a piece of early campaign strategy. Since the mayor's proposal for 2004 was leaked days ago, there has been lively debate in the press on whether holding the Olympic Games here would help solve some of the city's many problems or aggravate them. The environment is a sensitive aspect, especially since the mayor is a member of the Green party. Might not another Olympic building boom choke the city with thousands upon thousands of additional tons of concrete, besides strangling it with even more traffic? There are also worries that, with the city focusing on the one-time mass events in 2000 and possibly in 2004, its chronic woes—traffic, public transit and other badly functioning services, and air pollution—will worsen.

The 1960 Olympics were an evolutionary jump in Rome's growth from the dolce vita capital of two million residents to a barely manageable metropolis of three million. A lot of construction work was done then, including a new nine-mile beltway, the Via Olimpica, linking peripheral sports installations in the city's north and southwest. The value of real estate near the new roadway multiplied almost overnight and spurred development of new upper-middle-class housing. A few new underpasses were built in central areas to unblock the worst traffic bottlenecks. I left for Nigeria from the already cramped Ciampino Airport on the New Appian Road, and when I returned to Rome several months later my flight landed at the brand-new Fiumicino Airport near the sea.

The 1960 Olympics brought a lot of money to Rome and provided much free publicity for the city. If older Romans remember anything about the athletic side of the 1960 event, it's the lithe figure of Wilma G. Rudolph, the African-American runner who won three gold medals—for the 100- and 200-meter dashes and the

400-meter relay race, helping popularize track and field athletics in soccer-mad Italy. Rudolph was loved here, and there was genuine mourning in Rome when she died recently.

Spokespersons for local businesses voice enthusiasm for Mayor Rutelli's initiative. "This is perfect," said Maria Pia Marchetti, who heads the Federation of Small and Medium Industries. "After the Holy Year, we shall be ready for the Olympics. Among other things, we will be able to complete the facilities that we won't succeed in making function by 2000." The lady evidently knows about the delays and unkept promises bedeviling public-works projects.

Even the leader of right-wing opposition in the city parliament, Guido Anderson, for once supported the mayor: "We like his idea. This will be an opportunity for mobilizing all of Rome's resources."

• Hotel Luxuries •

MARCH 8

Train conversations in Italy are often revealing; people will tell perfect strangers personal and professional things that they wouldn't mention to acquaintances. There are of course the inevitable boasts and fictions, but my travel companion yesterday, a man who said he was the chief accountant at one of the leading Rome hotels, sounded sincere. We were alone in a compartment of the Milan-Rome *rapido* after the passengers who had filled it earlier got off in Florence; the accountant had boarded the fast train in Bologna where, he said, he had been on business.

He told me that Rome's luxury hotels, including the one at which he worked, were half empty and groaning under ruinous overheads, taxes, and heavy debt loads. "We all are practically broke," he confided.

It's still the off-season, I said, business would surely improve in Easter week next month. "The mobs that come to Rome for Easter don't stay in top establishments," my fellow passenger replied. "The city now has eight hundred hotels, and many are very plain but also comparatively cheap; besides, lots of monasteries take in paying guests, usually *carovane*." The Italian word for *caravan* means travel group in local hotel jargon. "We too take *carovane* now, which we never did before," the accountant went on, "but the travel agents who arrange accommodations for them want us to cut rates to the bone. We do it, just to fill rooms, but there is hardly any profit. Quality guests—there are fewer and fewer of them—resent *carovane*. International firms send their executives to business hotels where they obtain corporate rates. Our maids, waiters, and bellmen complain they get almost no tips anymore."

One doesn't read such sobering business reports in the local newspapers. They always tell their readers that wealthy foreigners beat a path to the finest hotels in the most beautiful city on earth.

Whenever I am asked, I say there are really only four luxury hotels in Rome—the Grand, the Excelsior, the Hassler, and the Lord Byron. The first three have been in operation for generations. The dowager of the top hotels, where the government still houses official visitors, was originally named Le Grand Hôtel et de Rome. It was built more than a hundred years ago at the behest of Prime Minister Marquess de Rudinì, a Sicilian conservative who thought that the capital of recently unified Italy needed a world-class hotel. He talked King Umberto I into helping raise the necessary funds. For the solemn opening of the Grand in 1894 its promoters signed up the legendary hotelier César Ritz and the no less famous chef Auguste Escoffier, then both in London.

When I first came to Rome, the most exalted guest at the Grand was the exiled former King Alfonso XIII of Spain. He lived in the hotel for ten years until his death in 1941. The Romans were convinced he was a *jettatore*, a person afflicted with the evil eye who would bring misfortune to people who associated with him. There were countless anecdotes of chandeliers crashing to the ground as he entered a hall, and of women's pearl necklaces snapping the moment they saw the ex-monarch, if only from afar. When he went to see a movie at the Quirinetta, his favorite cinema, near the Corso, half of the spectators would walk out for fear of a mishap.

I once mentioned Alfonso XIII to the owner of the Stella d'Italia (now the Marconi), a small hotel near the railroad terminal, where I worked at the reception desk for a few months following my arrival in Rome as a penniless émigré. The boss, a genial Sicilian, touched his crotch—an ancient gesture to ward off the sinister influence of a *jettatore*—and earnestly reprimanded me: "Never pronounce that name again! If you must speak about him at all— you'd better not—say something like 'the former sovereign of a southern European nation.'"

Cardinal Spellman, who worked at the Vatican as a young priest, loved the Grand. When he was archbishop of New York and a prince of the church he made frequent trips to Rome and usually stayed at the opulent establishment. He might have lived comfortably in the rectory of his titular church, Santi Giovanni e Paolo, near the Colosseum, which at his expense had been thoroughly restored in 1949. However, His Eminence joked, he couldn't afford to put up there because the good fathers in charge of the church would always come up with new ideas for extensive and costly work projects in the ancient edifice and the important archeological excavation area beneath it.

Aristocrats and diplomats still favor the Grand. It's also the only place in Rome where one can have tea between five and seven P.M. to the discreet sounds produced by a lady harpist. She plays in a corner of Le Grand Bar, a stuccoed hall with damask draperies and matching armchairs, while a frock-coated waiter serves tea in a nineteenth-century service.

Nearly equal in aplomb is the Hassler, which was opened at the upper end of the Spanish Stairs by Caroline and Albert Hassler in 1885. For some time it called itself the Hassler & New York, but during the Fascist dictatorship it was known as the Hotel Villa Medici because Mussolini had banned foreign-sounding business names (the twin-towered Villa Medici, nearby, has housed the French Academy since the age of Napoléon). For the last half century the hotel has been owned and run by the Bucher-Wirth family, a dynasty of Swiss hoteliers. I once saw President Truman step out of the Hassler one early morning, stop briefly at the parapet of the Spanish Stairs to take in the panorama of the Spanish Square below and of the Roman roofscape, and then briskly set out on his constitutional. Greeted by passersby, he courteously lifted his fedora. Presidents Eisenhower and Kennedy also signed the Hassler's guest book; royalty, heads of state and prime ministers of various countries, film stars, and some of the world's richest people have stayed at the panoramic hostelry. Every one of its rooms and suites is furnished differently, some with authentic antiques; the newly decorated penthouse suites are among the most luxurious accommodations the city has to offer.

The Excelsior, despite its dolce vita fame, is no longer quite on the level of elegance of the first two houses. When the 327-room Riviera-style palace was opened in 1906, the Via Veneto didn't yet exist, and shepherds tended their flocks in the nearby fields. During the last stages of World War II the Excelsior became the billet first of the commander of the German troops that had occupied Rome after the Italian armistice in 1943, and then, when the city was liberated from the Nazis, of Allied generals and their staffs.

To me the birth of la dolce vita is indissolubly linked in memory with that evening at the Excelsior in 1949 when Ingrid Bergman checked in. Even the *New York Times* took note of the Swedish-born film star's surprise trip to Rome to join the Italian director Roberto Rossellini for more than just a movie project. I was, with scores of other reporters, at Ciampino Airport to see her arrive. Rossellini was there to receive her with flowers, and to drive her in an open car to the Excelsior. Motorized police escorted them, followed by a motorcade of journalists.

At the hotel I saw at last my chance for asking Bergman a few questions. I stepped into the elevator behind her and Rossellini. While I spoke to the couple, a fourth person, a young photographer who had also squeezed into the elevator, took one flash picture after another. I stopped at the entrance to the suite toward which Rossellini steered his guest and peered through the open door into a room that was filled with flowers.

The cameraman brashly followed the couple inside, and Rossellini at last lost his patience and, with the assistance of a hotel dick who suddenly materialized, threw the intruder out. I didn't know then that what I saw was the prototypical Roman paparazzo and his brazen means of operation. The term for the new species was coined years later by Fellini. *Paparazzo* is a name that you can find in the Rome telephone directory; maybe the director of *La Dolce Vita* picked it because he thought it suited his movie character, sounding as it does like a blend of *bacarozzo*, the Roman dialect word for cockroach, and *papaceo*, denoting a big mosquito.

There were a score of paparazzi outside the Excelsior and in its lobby about a year later when we were waiting for the arrival of the shah of Iran, Mohammed Reza Pahlavi, and his empress, who had fled from Teheran after a coup d'état by Mohammed Mossadegh. We had learned at the last moment that the couple had landed at Ciampino Airport and were to put up at the then glamourous hotel. The shah looked greenish with fatigue, and Empress Soraya's dress suit was torn—a sign of how precipitous their departure into exile had been.

I was again at the Excelsior one early morning in 1953 when the shah and Empress Soraya were returning to Teheran after Mossadegh had been slain in an uprising that was later said to have been engineered by the Central Intelligence Agency of the United States. The shah said good-bye to us in a condescending manner; a colleague of mine who flew with him to Teheran told me later that as the chartered airplane was approaching Iran the shah went to a restroom, got into his gold-embroidered military uniform, and strode out, every inch the monarch. Soraya was often seen in Rome later after the shah had divorced her. She was an ex-empress who rarely smiled.

Located at the highest point of a quiet street in the affluent Parioli section in the city's north, the Lord Byron Hotel is much more exclusive today than when it was first opened after World War II. Designed in the 1930s as a private residence, the establishment was restructured and upgraded in the 1980s. Rooms were combined to make bigger units, and the interiors were lavishly redecorated. The Lord Byron now has just twenty-eight rooms and nine suites. Service is discreet and attentive, and the hotel hosts the superposh restaurant Le Jardin, the only one in Rome with two stars in the Michelin Guide of Italy.

If what my travel companion told me yesterday is true, I can't figure out how the four top hotels and the half dozen other houses that are almost on the same level of luxury can maintain their standards. Maybe the current devaluation of the lira, which makes Italy less expensive for hard-currency visitors, will help for a while.

• Marathon Debut •

A marathon, demonstratively patterned on the five-borough footrace held in New York City every fall, made its debut here today as a spectacular pre-spring happening. The cloudless, brisk Sunday morning favored the runners and brought out many more people, including myself, than are usually in Rome's streets on a day of rest. I joined crowds of tourists to watch the athletes at various points of their intricate racecourse.

About 4,500 men and women started from the Colosseum for the regulation twenty-six miles and 385 yards (41.3 kilometers, to the Romans). Nearly ten thousand others tried a separate, noncompetitive circuit of four and two-thirds miles, but many of them soon dropped out. There was also a short circuit for a race of wheelchair users. Mayor Francesco Rutelli, forty-two years old, donned a gray sweatsuit with the number 5,925 on his chest, jogged the entire shorter itinerary, and looked close to exhaustion when he arrived at the finishing line. The four men of the municipal police force's athletic squad who had run with him were in better shape.

The marathon course was designed to include some of the most famous squares, monuments, and vistas of Rome—clearly to get appealing footage for television. The City Hall promoters had granted exclusive coverage to the highest bidder, a nationwide private network. The state broadcasting system was miffed and completely ignored the Rome event on its video and radio channels all day; foreign networks, however, used clips, which was what the city most desired—excellent publicity for Rome as a travel and sight-seeing destination.

The marathon and the shorter races for joggers and wheelchair contenders both started and ended at the Colosseum, where thousands of cheering spectators filled the grandstands outside the ancient ruin. The main circuit went through the straight Via del Corso to the Piazza del Popolo and along the Tiber to the northern outskirts, turned around toward the Villa Borghese gardens, descended to the Spanish Square, took in the Piazza Navona, bordered the ruined Baths of Caracalla and the foot of Capitol Hill, and in its home stretch returned to the Colosseum through the Via dei Fori Imperiali with the Roman Forum on its south side.

A major spaghetti firm was the main commercial sponsor of the event and milked it relentlessly with signs, balloons, an inflatable triumphal arch spanning the Via del Babuino, and frequent spots interrupting the four-hour television special. Mobile video cameras provided glimpses of courtyards, swimming pools, penthouses, and roof gardens at the city center that one doesn't usually see otherwise.

Sports experts and popular entertainers worked as television commentators; I watched them mugging for the cameras in the Spanish Square. The Spanish Steps were filled with people who seemed more thrilled by the show business personalities than by the runners passing in the piazza below, where police and volunteers had a hard time keeping a narrow corridor open for them.

The city said that thirteen hundred men and women of its police force with more than 150 cars and motorcycles were on duty to keep order during the races and to divert traffic. Motorists had been warned to stay away from the city core this morning. Ambulances were stationed at various points of the course, and two thousand volunteers were also deployed.

Today's event was a first for Rome, though during the 1960 Summer Olympic Games in the city a marathon was run on a different, much less twisted, circuit. It was won by an Ethiopian, Abebe Bikila, who ran barefoot in 2 hours, 15 minutes, and 16.2 seconds.

Another Ethiopian was the winner today, the twenty-nine-year-old police sergeant Tadesse Belayneh, who wore state-of-the-art running shoes and finished in 2 hours, 10 minutes, and 13 seconds, close to the Olympic record. The runner-up, 11 seconds behind, was a Tanzanian, Salum Kaji, who lives in northern Italy. The first Italian, Salvatore Nicosia, was fifth; the winning female runner was Yelena Sipatova of Russia, who is thirty-nine years old. The last runner to complete the entire race was a doctor; he made it in six hours and seventeen minutes.

Today's main race was officially called "Roma City Marathon" (in English), evidence that the New York classic—in which many Italians take part year after year—is the avowed model. What's more, officials of the New York City Marathon were here today as guests of Rome. One television commentator remarked that if The Big Apple was unsurpassed in its perfect organization of the annual race, Rome was able to offer a scenery of antiquities and other sights such as no city on earth could match.

• Looting Industry •

MARCH 17
_____

We were again reminded today that trafficking in looted archeological objects and art treasures is a lucrative industry here. Efforts to recover a precious wooden statuette of the Virgin and child from the thirteenth century, stolen from a village church, resulted in the discovery of a ring of thieves and fences in Rome who are believed to have supplied international dealers with art plunder.

The medieval wood carving had first disappeared from the Church of Saint Martin at Vico del Lazio, fifty-six miles south of here, in 1975, but it was quickly retrieved. The police allege that British or Swiss middlemen had expressed continuing interest in the wooden Madonna, and had commissioned Roman racketeers to get it after all. Exactly a year ago the statuette vanished again from the church in a nighttime break-in.

Apparently acting on a tip from an informer or on the basis of wiretaps, the police during the last few days raided a farm building near Fiumicino, the old fishing village that has lent its name to the adjacent main airport of Rome, and found the missing Virgin and child. The wood sculpture, wrapped in a bedsheet, was in a cardboard box, ready for shipping.

One thing led to another, and in searches of various homes and other caches in and around Rome more than two thousand archeological items were seized—Greek, Etruscan, and Roman vases and amphorae; chunks of marble statuaries; and other ancient artifacts. The loot is said to have come from the Roman Forum and other excavation sites in and near the city, from museums, and from clandestine digs. Criminal charges were brought against sixteen persons.

Police officers have told me on various occasions that hundreds of people in Rome, some of them academically trained or self-styled scholars, are implicated on a permanent basis in the illegal commerce with art and antiquities. A number of years ago, on an assignment, I spoke to one of these characters—a highly educated American—about some ancient pottery that according to Italian authorities had been smuggled out of this country and had turned up in collections in the United States.

Since then the trafficking seems to have been going on unabated. An average of four archeological or art objects are stolen in Italy every day of the year, and Rome is reputed to be a center for storing the plunder and eventually disposing of it. Pieces of ancient Roman statues may end up adorning the living rooms of private homes here or elsewhere in Italy; more conspicuous or valuable stolen objects are shipped by devious ways to

Zurich or London, where they can easily be sold. Thus the box with the wooden Madonna and child from Vico del Lazio might soon have been hidden under a load of Sicilian oranges on a truck bound for Switzerland.

Of course there is much to steal in the Eldorado of art thieves. Understaffed and underfunded museums in Rome and elsewhere in Italy have trouble guarding the treasures in their showrooms and seem to have forgotten about all the ancient jugs, cups, helmets, weapons, belt buckles, and other items filling their storerooms. Paintings and statues abound in Rome's hundreds of churches as well as in towns and villages around the city. Burglar alarms, where they exist, are routinely disconnected by experienced looters. There is no overall inventory of historic and artistic treasures in Rome, let alone in all of Italy.

Each of the three rival main branches of the national police forces—the Carabinieri, the state police, and the finance guard—has its own agenda for tracking stolen art; there isn't much, if any, coordination among them. Each of the three competing law enforcement agencies runs its own informers and conducts its own investigations, principally interested, it seems, in getting exclusive credit on television and in the press for any success.

Thus, the newspapers today carried photos of the thirteenth-century Madonna and some of the ancient vases and other pottery recovered in the latest sweep, displayed on a large table like a buffet spread. The most conspicuous feature of the pictures were two men in flak jackets with GUARDIA DI FINANZA (Finance Guard) in large letters across their chests. There was no danger of the two officers being fired at when the camera people were called in, but the bulletproof apparel of the fiscal police added drama—and let there be no mistake as to who had discovered the loot!

A captain of the Carabinieri art recovery squad at its handsome rococo building in the Piazza di Sant' Ignazio told me recently that the kingpins of the illegal international trade in stolen antiquities and works of art were not only hand and glove with looters but also with forgers: "The racketeers seem to have no trouble marketing the phony amphorae, statues, and paintings turned out by copyists." The captain added with what sounded like patriotic pride: "Some of our fakers are genuine artists in their field. A few of their counterfeit objects are still being shown as authentic in museums in Germany, Britain, and America."

• Saint Joseph's Pastry •

MARCH 19

The neighborhood celebrations that used to spice the Roman year seem to be losing their flavor. Today's Saint Joseph festival in the Trionfale section, at any rate, was a tired affair. Until a few years ago people from all over the city would flock to our district on this day, some for worship in the Church of San Giuseppe, others for the fresh pastry they could buy from outdoor vendors.

In the 1950s when I was a newcomer to this area it was still crowded all day on March 19, the feast day of Saint Joseph. Sidewalk stands where chunks of sweetened dough were being deep-fried in olive oil, coated with powdered sugar, and sold as *fritelle* were packed with customers. For the Trionfale section the foster father of Jesus was "San Giuseppe *fritellaro*," the fried-pastry Saint Joseph. Another sweet treat was *bigné* (a corruption of the French word *beignet*, fritter), cream puffs that were sold by the thousands in the confectioners' shops near the parish church and devoured on the spot. Frascati wine was drunk convivially at the sidewalk tables of the trattorias, weather permitting.

Little of that Saint Joseph's Day atmosphere has survived in our corner of the city. The confectioners, it is true, were doing good business today with their *bigné* (now $1.20 apiece), but most of the buyers had them wrapped and hurried home, probably to watch the soccer games on television. Today was a Sunday, and Italy was also observing Father's Day.

City Hall as usual had sent us the mobile decorations for streets that are scheduled to be the scene of solemnities. The Trionfale section received a truckload of arches, formed by strips of thin wood and studded with colored lightbulbs; I suppose the current for the illumination a few hours last night and again tonight was paid for by the city. Tomorrow the flimsy triumphal arches that tonight are still spanning a couple of our streets will be dismantled again.

Early this afternoon a patrol car of the municipal police with four officers turned up; City Hall must have had an inkling that no big crowd was expected for this year's Saint Joseph's Day. By three P.M. some five hundred people were standing and milling outside the Church of San Giuseppe. Its imposing revival baroque facade over a flight of stairs masks a barnlike brick building that went up in 1912; the freestanding brickwork campanile is crowned with an open bell loft surmounted by a larger-than-life gilt statue of Saint Joseph. I live five blocks from the church and hear the tower carillon at noon every day.

Just before four P.M. a detail of three young Carabinieri leisurely walked toward the church, visibly bored by their Sunday afternoon assignment. A procession formed. Half a dozen elderly sacristans with short red-and-white capes over their business suits, one of them carrying a large gilt cross, emerged from St. Joseph's. A brass band of uniformed boys and girls from the adjacent parochial school followed them, playing snappy marches instead of sacred hymns. Behind them came kindergarten tots holding hands, guided by nuns. They were followed in turn by the members of a laypersons' association, the women wearing white head scarves and mumbling the prayers that a gray-cowled monk led with a bullhorn.

After the laity came twenty or so students for the priesthood, all wearing white surplices over black cassocks and walking with their hands folded. A movable platform, its wheels concealed behind a kind of cloak reaching almost to the pavement, bore a fifteen-foot painted statue of Saint Joseph carrying the infant Jesus in his arms. The saint's metal halo swayed as young men in dark suits pushed the mobile pedestal.

The handful of priests who are the church's permanent clergy walked behind it, preceding a bishop with a miter on his head who made gestures of blessing left and right. Of course a mere bishop, even in full regalia, causes about as little stir in the city of the pope as a captain does at army headquarters teeming with top brass.

The people who had been waiting outside the church brought up the rear of the procession. I knew quite a few of them either personally or by sight; they were owners of stores in our area or neighbors. Nurses and patients looked out of many windows of the clinic on the right side of the church, and some showered confetti on the parade. The clinic and some windows of the apartment houses nearby were adorned with little pieces of pink or purple tapestry.

To the delight of the kindergarten detachment, a large German shepherd, upset by the big saint's statue and its unsteady halo, barked furiously from its third-floor balcony vantage point.

Our neighborhood soon relapsed into its normal Sunday afternoon inertia. I didn't see any *fritelle* fryer; nor had the trattorias bothered to put out tables and chairs, but the Trionfale district became livelier again later when euphoric Lazio fans returned from the Olympic Stadium where their team had humiliated the visiting Genoa, four to nought.

March

• Unwanted Newcomers •

It took me forty minutes in a rented car this morning to find the Via Prenestina, the ancient highway leading to Palestrina. I had to visit an American friend who had settled in the historic town (it may be older than Rome). The reason for my slow progress wasn't just heavy traffic; I also took a few wrong turns because the eastern outskirts of Rome had become as strange to me as if I were driving in a modern section of Tunis. I hadn't been in the district of the Italian capital for a couple of years and found completely new neighborhoods had sprung up in once-seedy areas—high-rise buildings on new streets with names I had never heard before, shopping centers, and bus routes with unfamiliar numbers.

When I first saw the flat expanse between the highways to Tivoli and Naples—there were no expressways then—it was still mostly rural, with sheep grazing on vast patches between truck farms. Mussolini had just ordered clusters of tenements erected here and there to house thousands of poor Romans whom he had banned from the historic center. Large-scale demolitions were underway in the city core to clear spaces for projects that were supposed to add grandeur to the capital of the new Fascist empire.

The concrete boxes, some of them three stories tall, that were to be the new homes for the people exiled from the heart of Rome were called *borgate* (suburban hamlets). Their inhabitants had to ride two or three buses twice a day to get to and from jobs in the city or for shopping expeditions. There were few if any markets, stores, restaurants, espresso bars, post offices, schools, or clinics in the new *borgate*; they soon became outright slums.

During World War II their population was swollen by refugees from Naples and other southern cities and towns that were targets of frequent Allied air raids and from the villages near Monte-cassino that had become battlefields.

Mussolini's new *borgate* started spawning a belt of rickety hous-ing and shacks like evil outgrowths. One of the first to explore the squalor of the eastern outskirts was Pier Paolo Pasolini, the poet, writer, and film director. A northerner who had moved to Rome, he focused on the sprawling *borgate* about which most natives of the capital knew nothing and didn't want to hear. Pasolini por-trayed the suburban slums as a breeding ground of petty crime and prostitution where nevertheless human warmth, decency, and love were also present. Pasolini was slain in another outlying area, near Fiumicino Airport, in 1975 by a male prostitute from the *borgate* whom he had picked up outside Rome's railroad terminal. The murderer was arrested; he confessed and served a prison term.

Driving today through the eastern suburbs with their rows after rows of housing complexes marching toward the hills of Tivoli and Frascati, I thought that some of these developments might have been transplanted from Bucharest. These new Roman neighborhoods are unlovely, yet they are Roman too, I quickly noticed—the packs of motor scooters ignoring red lights, the jay-walkers, the relative stylish way people dress even though they may affect a trashy look, the crowds in the espresso shops.

Since the 1980s, the A and B lines of the Metropolitana, the subway, between which eastern Rome is spreading, have made it easier for *borgate* residents to reach the city center, although they may have to take a bus to the nearest station. Some people living in older neighborhoods say it was a big mistake to build the Metropolitana because it enables the *borgatari* (the local term for suburban rowdies) to get to the Spanish Square in half an hour and to horse around in the swanky Via Condotti and jostle respectable folk along the Corso. It's like hearing Parisians bad-mouthing the *banlieusards* (most of whom are North Africans), or Manhattanites condescending to the bridge-and-tunnel crowd from the other boroughs, Long Island, and New Jersey.

Urban planners drawing up a comprehensive zoning map in 1962 decided that the rolling plains between the older residential districts on Rome's east and the hills was the area where the city should further expand; above all, it should provide the space for relocating government departments from Rome's congested heart.

The vision of a new Rome east of the existing one—comparable to the modern La Défense district on the western outskirts of Paris—has been kept alive for more than three decades, but nothing has happened so far to translate it into reality. The mega-project has little more to show so far than an official name, *Sistema Direzionale Orientale* (Eastern Directional System), or SDO for short.

Phalanxes of government workers, ensconced in some old palazzo in the city center, love to saunter out around ten A.M. for their cappuccino or to do some shopping and dread the thought of being transferred to a distant bureaucratic citadel near the crumbling arch of a ruined aqueduct that furnished water to the Rome of the Caesars. Alas, the city is taking the first meaningful steps to prepare for such a civil service exodus. On the basis of a decision reached by the municipal government last fall, City Hall is surveying areas on the eastern outskirts suitable for large-scale construction projects. The 1962 zoning plan has been modified so as to leave ample room for public and archeological parks. The old aqueducts aren't the only relics from antiquity east of the historic city walls. The subsoil and the soft tufa rocks hold ancient tombs; remains of ancient Roman buildings, medieval churches, and other old structures are everywhere.

City Hall also aired a proposal the other day to erect the city's first skyscraper as an architectural symbol of Rome's twenty-first-century dynamism. Details are still vague, but the structure must be invisible from the historic center, although I would probably see its tip on the eastern horizon from my windows if there isn't too much smog, as would the tourists who climb the dome of St. Peter's.

The mayor suggested that the first Roman skyscraper might be shaped like a giant obelisk (a dozen Egyptian obelisks rise in various spots in and near the city center). There are indications that the extra-high structure, whatever its outline, would be built near the present Tiburtina station, a suburban railroad hub and subway stop with a new terminal for long-distance buses nearby. The idea is to have the state railways and possibly other semipublic agencies use part of the projected landmark and to get private tenants for the remaining office space at what ought to become a prestigious address.

Does Rome, of all cities, need a skyscraper? The project is inevitably stirring a heated public debate. Urbanists, art critics, architects, ecologists, sociologists, and sundry commentators are already making themselves heard for or against; the dissonant chorus will swell if the proposal to greet the next millennium in Rome with a steel, concrete, and glass ziggurat gathers support.

As it is, I found the eastern outskirts still unappealing when I was driving to Palestrina and back today. Where there are no stark high-rises, the district is cluttered with car wreckers' lots, deposits for building materials, truck sheds, mechanical shops, and a few sports fields. There are also some unkempt stretches where gypsies are encamped. I wasn't surprised to notice Mercedeses and BMWs side by side with battered campers and trailers, amid laundry strung up to dry and flocks of small children and mangy-looking dogs. Gypsies driving expensive cars have long become a theme of metropolitan folklore here, yet Mayor Rutelli professed astonishment the other day when he was passing a gypsy camp on the southwestern outskirts and spotted a flaming red Ferrari parked there. Such fast cars, when new, cost more than $100,000; as antiques they may fetch much higher prices from collectors. The mayor asked the police to investigate. A twenty-three-year-old immigrant from the former Yugoslavia was found to be the owner of the Ferrari—a pimpmobile, or the indulgence of a young drug baron? The registration seemed in order, but the police impounded the car anyway on some formality.

A few days later a strong Carabinieri unit raided the camp at dawn, searching every vehicle. They seized automatic weapons, plenty of handguns, and $50,000 worth of jewelry—chains, bracelets, gold watches, and other items—that the authorities believe to be spoils from thefts and robberies.

Episodes like these aren't likely to improve the strained relations between a large part of the Roman populace and the two or three thousand gypsies encamped on the city's outskirts. During the daytime, groups of gypsy women in flowing skirts who want to read your hand or little bands of begging gypsy children have long become a common sight in the city center, especially in areas much visited by tourists. Clashes between suburban tenement dwellers and the nomads have been frequent lately, to the dismay of civil rights advocates. The gypsy population around Rome has grown sizably since the collapse of Yugoslavia, causing new problems that nobody here seems to know how to solve.

• Diplomatic Trouble •

MARCH 31

Two Zairean diplomats fought with an Italian in the garden of a villa on the Monte Mario the other day; there were black eyes and bruises on both sides. A policeman on guard duty outside the gate was unable to intervene because the premises are extraterritorial, and law enforcement officers of the host country may set foot in them only following a request by the foreign mission's chief—which didn't materialize.

I know the Zairean-occupied villa because I pass it whenever I visit friends who live nearby on the hill. I think I would recognize the Roman involved in yesterday's brawl: he is the owner of the building and landlord of the Zaireans. He must be the grim-looking man who some months ago led a sit-in outside his own property; with him were other local people who claim to have had trouble with foreign diplomats and want the privileges of those guests curbed. I read the posters that the hapless landlord had put up on utility poles in the neighborhood; they asserted that the Zaireans hadn't paid any rent for more than three years. Since diplomats don't have to obey a court summons in their host country, it is useless suing them; the Zaireans apparently continue paying no rent.

According to the press, the fight in the straggly garden of the villa on the Monte Mario prompted an outpouring of complaints about nonpaying foreign diplomats. Several embassies of notoriously broke or strife-ridden nations are in arrears with rentals and the salaries of their local help. Foreign diplomats often ignore bills from stores and stiff physicians, lawyers, and other professionals; if a plumber is called into a diplomatic mission to fix a broken pipe, he is likely to request cash even before opening his toolbox. The municipal police have long given up writing tickets for cars with diplomatic license plates because they know that the fines for double-parking, speeding, or other violations would never be paid.

It's a problem vexing also Washington, New York, and other world centers. Rome, however, is particularly bedeviled by it because this capital is housing more diplomatic missions than almost any other city on earth—more than two hundred. Many countries maintain two separate embassies here, one to the Italian Republic and one to the Holy See (as the Vatican is called when its formal relations with other states are involved). What's more, several foreign envoys to the United Nations Food and Agriculture Organization, which has its seat here, and to the Order of Malta, also headquartered in Rome, have diplomatic status too. In all, some thirteen thousand foreigners enjoy diplomatic privileges in the Italian capital and thus may get away with, say, running a red light or flouting laws and obligations in more serious ways.

Of course the majority of diplomats, particularly those of major powers, make a point of giving no offense. They also spend a lot of money here in luxury stores, restaurants, and nightspots; when they entertain they use the services of local caterers, spend their foreign-service allowances pleasurably, and may even pay social security contributions for their Italian employees.

Over the years as a foreign correspondent here I have met a cross section of the diplomatic corps in Rome, and some of its members have become friends. Many embassy officials are very busy, well informed, and convinced they are doing useful work. Others lead a vapid existence in a dream job, drifting from one gossipy diplomatic party to the next or playing golf at the hundred-year-old Acqua Santa Club between the Ancient Appian Way and the Via Appia Nuova. A few are busy writing their memoirs.

April

• Wasp Woes •

<u>APRIL 6</u>

The new Association for Pedestrians' Rights issued a manifesto against "traffic violence" today, appealing to the authorities and to the public to make Rome again "a city where one can at least survive." The group represents a growing local current in the broad environmental movement. In about the same way as the nationwide antitobacco lobby calls for the protection of nonsmokers from secondary nicotine fumes, the pedestrians' association claims the sidewalks for exclusive use by citizens on foot and claims the right to cross the streets without having to fear for one's life.

Today's document denounced the invasion of spaces that should be reserved for pedestrians by motor scooters, illegally parked cars, and sidewalk vendors; it didn't mention the outdoor tables of restaurants and cafés, or the dog walkers who don't clean up the messes left by their pets (I have never seen one dog lover here who did).

The pedestrians' protest must have been prompted by the sudden increase in traffic density during the last few days as Easter is approaching. High season in Rome's tourist business starts around this time; this year the devaluation of the Italian lira appears to have encouraged more foreigners to visit this country and its capital. The traffic patterns in Rome's center and in a vast area around it are so delicate that the appearance of an additional hundred tourist coaches from the Italian provinces and from abroad is apt to choke the city.

The current traffic woes are deepening worries about what the Holy Year 2000 of the Roman Catholic Church may do to the city. The religious jubilee threatens to become a "festival of urban congestion," warns the chairwoman of the Association for Pedestrians' Rights, Flavia Schreiber.

The traffic bottlenecks exasperate motorists, raise the already high levels of air pollution, and cause a racket of car horns many hours a day; yet the main hazard for pedestrians is motor scooters.

The Piaggio Company of Pontedera near Pisa was prophetic when, soon after World War II, it called a new motor scooter model *Vespa* (wasp). The two-wheel insects have proliferated beyond the firm's boldest expectations. Like swarms of angry wasps, hundreds of thousands of scooters buzz all over the city today. They aren't only Vespas but also various other makes; Francesco Rutelli was driving a Honda SH50 before he became mayor of Rome and started riding in a limousine with bodyguards. Rome in fact may be the world capital of motor scooters, mopeds, and motorcycles—more than 800,000 are in circulation, almost one for every three residents.

A committee of the European Union found in a study recently that motor scooters were helping ease urban traffic problems. The Brussels experts did not seem to have considered the performance of Rome's vast tribe of—mostly youthful—*vespistas* who have developed riding a two-wheel motor vehicle into urban guerrilla tactics. They pass cars on their left or right to cut a few inches in front of them, surge in packs of a dozen or more into intersections regardless of traffic lights, turn without warning, take the wrong direction in one-way streets, and frighten people by coming up on the sidewalk behind them or shooting out of a lateral lane. Only the quick reactions with which many Italians are endowed prevent more accidents than actually happen every day.

Pedestrians often curse the anarchic scooterists, only to have one of the Roman vernacular's foul epithets shouted back to them over a quickly widening distance.

Motor scooters and motorcycles are the favorite tools of the city's redoubtable brigade of chain grabbers and bag snatchers, who usually operate in pairs. Two-wheel mobility "favors street crime and teaches young people to violate the law," says Gianfranco di Pretoro, an ecologist, in a report on urban traffic.

The whining and roar of Vespas and their cousins also contribute to the din in Rome's streets. Motor scooters come from the manufacturers with mufflers to keep their noise to within 71 decibels, a limit set by European Union rules. Young owners almost always have the sound-abatement device removed and other alterations made to improve the engine performance and, of course, heighten the noise. Do-it-yourself kits to soup up motor scooters and motorbikes can be bought at spare parts shops all over town.

Even motor scooters that aren't in operation at the moment cause inconvenience. Any number of them are parked on sidewalks; fastened with thick chains to iron gates, railings, and utility poles; clustered in metal thickets particularly outside office buildings, schools, markets, stores, and cinemas. Despite the chains and heavy locks, scores of motor scooters are stolen every day; the thieves, wielding heavy-duty steel shears, usually pick the latest models from the bunch.

If one turns to the police, the desk sergeant will add the theft report to a stack of previous ones and warn the complainant that the chances for recovery are slim. For employees and students who tend to sleep late in the morning as well as for messengers, reporters, couriers, and other people in a hurry, the trusty Vespa is nevertheless a means to get quickly to where they are supposed to go. Such mobility comes at a price.

• Trattoria Transparency •

APRIL 9

City Hall decreed yesterday that eating places in Rome may no longer automatically add bread-and-cover charges to what they ask their patrons to pay. This means, at last, a welcome departure from bad old habits in a city that depends substantially on tourist business, and where eating out is a cherished way of socializing for many residents.

The item *pane e coperto*, often preprinted at the top of restaurant checks, amounted lately to the equivalent of $1.50 to $2.50 per person. This fixed charge had baffled generations of foreign visitors, particularly if they hadn't partaken of the rolls and breadsticks that were routinely put on their tables; they were also puzzled by having to shell out a special fee for the privilege of using the establishment's plates, cutlery, and napkins—were they supposed to eat with their hands?

Of course now the prices for meals will go up as restaurants conceal the former bread-and-cover charge in the figures for single dishes, maybe in the pasta course with which most people here start lunch or dinner. In some places patrons will have to account for each piece of bread they take.

The city's commerce commissioner, Claudio Minelli, explains that what is wanted is "transparency" in the price structure of trattorias. To achieve this, he also outlawed the practice by which many restaurants, especially the pricier ones, mark their menu listings for seafood and fine meats with a code rather than with a specific price. The foreigners have always been at a loss to puzzle out what "*Rombo, s.g.*" or "*Bistecca fiorentina, s.q.*" might mean. They don't often realize that it is "Turbot, according to size" or "Florentine steak, depending on quantity." Or the bill of fare would sometimes inform patrons of the price for a meat dish, noting "*p.e.*" This was supposed to mean *per etto* (for 100 grams). Even if diners could decipher such menu mysteries, they wouldn't be likely to march into the kitchen, armed with a measuring stick or a pocket balance, to check sizes or weights of the treats they ordered.

The city's move for trattoria transparency has won endorsement by the Chamber of Commerce and, reluctantly, also by the Restaurant Owners' Association. It's the first reform in fifteen years in the age-old ways of Roman restauranteering. In the early 1980s the central government made the so-called fiscal receipt compulsory for all establishments providing food and drink; that was a major revolution. Since then restaurants must give their patrons checks on blanks that the tax office has previously stamped and numbered; the fiscal receipt must contain the restaurant owner's name, address, and taxpayer's identification number and must detail each course and beverage charged to the customer. Restaurant guests are supposed to keep their checks on them for at least a little while because inspectors may be lurking outside the premises and requesting to see what has been paid.

The idea is to enable the fiscal authorities to ascertain the actual cash flow of a given business and make sure that value-added tax (a kind of sales tax) on the price of every restaurant meal is paid. When the fiscal receipt was introduced we in Rome all recalled the old Italian adage *fatta la legge, trovato l'inganno*, which means that as soon as a new law is enacted, ways to get around it are discovered. Yet the fiscal receipt has stuck and has become a way of restaurant life.

True enough, in years of patronizing Roman restaurants week after week, I have been requested to produce a fiscal receipt only once. Two plainclothes officers of the Guardia di Finanza, the fiscal police, stopped me outside *La Pollarola* near the Campo de' Fiori where I had entertained two friends, and wanted to see the check. *La Pollarola* is an unassuming place, fancied among others by junior diplomats of the nearby French Embassy; the management knows better than to fiddle with checks. I had left ours by mistake on the plate when I had paid, and sheepishly said so to the inspectors. They went inside to see if this was true. If there hadn't been any fiscal receipt, both the manager of *La Pollarola* and I would have been liable for fines.

On the other hand, I never get a fiscal receipt at the small Sicilian place near the Tiber where I have lunch at least once a month because I like its extraordinary wine from the island's west coast. When I ask for the check, the matronly woman who runs the trattoria always sends me a small piece of paper of the kind one uses for lining drawers with just one figure scrawled on it in pencil; it's always a round sum, always gratifyingly low. I add a tip for the waiter and slink into the busy street outside, telling myself I couldn't really embarrass the friendly Sicilian hostess by requesting something so coldly official as a *ricevuta fiscale* (although she must keep the printed forms somewhere). If I am ever stopped by the Finance Guard I would have to play the uninformed foreigner who doesn't speak any Italian, or lie that I had just been saying hello to my old friend the restaurant manager without eating, drinking, or paying anything. But the robust red wine might be on my breath.

• Little Easter •

APRIL 17

Today is *Pasquetta*, "Little Easter," the lazy Monday after the feast of the Resurrection. In Italy it is a national holiday, and for the Church it is the anticlimactic Monday of the Angel. After eight days of paschal rites and pageantry, the Vatican was taking it easy today, and the pope flew by helicopter to his hillside residence of Castelgandolfo to recuperate from what to him must have been a period of considerable physical strain.

During such Easter ceremonies as I was attending or watching on television almost all the people who cheered the pontiff and received his blessings appeared to be visitors from other parts of Italy or from abroad. The cheap lira brought a bumper crop of foreigners. Out-of-towners and international tourists filled St. Peter's Square on Palm Sunday, April 9, and again on Easter Sunday yesterday. Where were the Romans?

Hundreds of thousands were spending the Easter holidays elsewhere, and most of them will straggle back late this afternoon and tonight while quite a few others, as every year, will stay away one more day or two. The Romans who remained in town didn't seem to care much for the pope or what he was doing and saying; at most they watched his appearances distractedly on the little screen for a few minutes while getting ready for lunch or dinner.

The Romans have of course been nonchalant about the pontiff—their own bishop—for centuries, and their religious attitudes have long been suspect to the Church. Rome is "no longer Christian," John Paul II's vicar for the city, Camillo Cardinal Ruini, complained recently. The ascetic-looking cardinal, himself a northerner, deplored that Rome was, according to him, pervaded by a "post-Christian mentality" that seemed quite pleasant and was shared also by people (including priests?) who assumed, quite wrongly, that they were within the Church. The pope's vicar didn't denounce anticlericalism, because there is little of that in this city.

Rome, deriving a lot of income from the presence of the papacy, doesn't openly oppose it. Militant freethinkers here would probably be appalled if the Vatican were to relocate to some other place in the world—the same way as Neapolitan Communists at the height of the Cold War protested when the North Atlantic Treaty Organization considered moving its Mediterranean Command from Naples.

If almost all Romans want the pope in their city, the degree of their religious convictions and piety is something else again. A poll conducted by a Catholic university team during the last few months found that scarcely one fourth of all nominal Catholics here attend Sunday Mass in one of the city's several hundred churches, and that only one out of every ten young adults professes to be a believer.

Thousands of young people did cheer the pope in St. Peter's Square on Palm Sunday, but almost all of them had come in church-organized group tours from the Italian provinces and other countries.

The many sidewalk vendors who sold palm fronds and olive twigs did most of their business with tourists who would take those symbols of peace, soon to be blessed by the pope, back home with them as souvenirs. John Paul II himself carried an olive twig on his bishop's staff, which he used for support as he was walking, his left hand clutching the shoulder of an ecclesiastical aide.

The pontiff was going through the Palm Sunday liturgy at a canopied altar that had been erected in front of St. Peter's, when a few hundred Romans arrived in the crowded piazza after having paraded across the city center in a protest against the death penalty. Italy has long abolished capital punishment; the civil rights groups that sponsored the march meant to denounce it in other countries. Few of the foreigners in St. Peter's Square appeared to be aware of the peaceful demonstration and what it was all about.

Nor did the pope directly acknowledge the protest. In his homily he reminded his listeners of the divine command "Thou shalt not kill," but he cited it to defend the renewed condemnation of abortion and euthanasia in his recent encyclical *Evangelium Vitae* (the Gospel of Life), against his many critics.

As I went home after the rite, I passed hawkers who displayed new sweatshirts with a color reproduction of Michelangelo's Creator transmitting life to Adam, as pictured on the ceiling of the Sistine Chapel; one would have preferred a warm jacket rather than a sweatshirt, despite the sunshine. Before noon a cold westerly wind had sprung up, auguring no good.

The weather worsened during Easter week. A cold rain came down most of Good Friday, and that night only about three thousand diehards were at the Colosseum to witness the pope carrying a large cross in a reenactment of the Passion of Jesus. In earlier years John Paul II had borne a wooden cross throughout the lengthy ceremony; this time he was prevailed upon by his entourage to shoulder a plastic cross, weighing no more than a few pounds, for only five minutes. Watching the pope on television,

I noticed that he appeared to walk with difficulty and looked bone-tired.

During the remaining episodes of the Stations of the Cross at the Colosseum a few handpicked persons relieved John Paul II of the symbolic burden he had carried; one of them was a woman, Minke de Vries, who belonged to a Protestant community in Switzerland—an ecumenical gesture and a nod toward female Catholics who demand a more conspicuous role in the church. The spectators huddled under dripping clumps of umbrellas, and everybody, including the pontiff, must have been glad when it was all over.

The sky wasn't much more clement on Easter Sunday. A cold rain was punctuated by squalls that ripped apart umbrellas. John Paul II officiated inside St. Peter's instead of in the square outside, as he had done in previous years. After Easter Mass, however, he stepped out on the central loggia and gave a speech in Italian, calling for reconciliation and peace in the various trouble spots around the globe—more or less what he was expected to say.

Before imparting his apostolic blessing the pope wished a "Happy Easter!" to the crowd in the square and to his broadcast audience in fifty-seven languages, a performance I find increasingly tedious each time it is repeated. A chilly downpour drove me to my favorite espresso bar in the Borgo section before the pontiff had concluded his linguistic exploit.

The Polish pope, despite his manifest health problems, surprises by his resilience. The radio just reported that he had prayed at noon with a few hundred pilgrims who had been taken to Castelgandolfo in coaches. When some of them shouted *"Viva il Papa!"* John Paul II good-naturedly responded, "Long live everybody!" The broadcast speaker said the pontiff was in "great form." Perhaps he was relieved that his Easter chores were done and that he too could enjoy *Pasquetta.*

The sun at last shone again today, if only timidly—hardly the weather for picnicking. When I first came to live in Rome, the Monday after Easter was the day for lunch *fuori porta* (outside the city gates), though even then the city had long spilled far beyond its ancient walls.

I remember a *Pasquetta* when we took a bus from the Colosseum to the Ancient Appian Way, and from the last stop walked for only ten minutes past the crowded outdoor tables of a rustic trattoria before we settled down in a grassy spot near the headless statue of a togaed Roman, marking the tomb of some ancient worthy. We feasted on cold chicken, drinking the wine we had brought with us in a straw-covered flask. All around us Roman families had spread out and mothers were yelling to gather their broods: "Mario, Silvana, stop running around, the pasta is getting cold!"

None of the people I know here seems to have gone picnicking *fuori porta* today. One family drove to the Alps on Good Friday for some late-season skiing; they will have found plenty of snow. Other neighbors signed up with a travel agency for a trip to Paris, where today they will probably be queuing with thousands of other tourists to get into the Louvre Museum. The mass-travel industry also provides similar delights in Rome. When I passed the Walls of Michelangelo on my way to St. Peter's Square or the city center during the last few days, the line for the Vatican Museums was at least a third of a mile long.

• The She-Wolf •

APRIL 21

Today is officially the 2,747th anniversary of Rome's foundation, but the occasion passed almost unobserved. During the Fascist dictatorship, *Natale di Roma*, the birthday of Rome, was a national holiday that produced an orgy of oratory by Mussolini and his lieutenants. Today a few local dailies mentioned the historical significance of the date by force of habit, and working Romans knocked off early from their jobs to prepare for an extra-long weekend made possible by a legal holiday next Tuesday.

There weren't even the usual newspaper cartoons depicting a pair of politicians or some other unpopular figures as the mythical twins, Romulus and Remus, sucking taxpayers' money from a disgruntled she-wolf supposedly representing the Treasury.

The legend that a she-wolf suckled the exposed infant twins who eventually would establish a walled settlement on the Palatine Hill, the future Rome, is very old. However, the traditional date for the city's birth, 753 B.C., is arbitrary and probably two centuries too remote. The day, April 21, is that of an ancient spring festival that may not have had anything to do with the city.

The Capitoline She-Wolf, the bronze sculpture in the Palace of the Conservatori, is about 2,500 years old. Scholars are for once in general agreement that it is the work of an Etruscan artist of the fifth century B.C.; thanks to a hint by Pliny the Elder they even have a name for him: Vulca of Veii. He or his disciples are believed to have turned out the She-Wolf in a foundry in the then-flourishing city of Veii (in the countryside north of Rome where the authorities had illegal housing bulldozed last September).

The haunting She-Wolf is my favorite sculpture, full of mystery and potential dread. It stirs me more deeply than does any statuary of classical gods, goddesses, and heroes I have seen anywhere, more even than do Michelangelo's *Pietà* in St. Peter's and *Moses* in the Church of San Pietro in Vincoli. Every now and then I climb the steps up the Capitoline Hill to visit the She-Wolf once again. The time I have spent over the years standing in the Hall of the She-Wolf staring at the archaic masterpiece must add up to hours.

The representation of the sharply observed animal is realistic and at the same time stylized. The lean, sinewy She-Wolf turns her head to the left as if sensing possible danger. Her jaws are half open, baring her fangs as if she were about to growl, howl, or snap. Back, neck, and head form a bent horizontal line, nearly level. The ears are pricked up to catch suspicious sounds, the eyes suggest distrust. The ribs are visible under the She-Wolf's naked flanks, her coat suggested only on her neck, back, and tail and by strings running down her shoulders. Her legs are sturdy, her udders plump—she must have whelped recently.

The Etruscan sculptor presumably put the mythical twins below the She-Wolf; if so, they have been lost. The present Romulus and Remus are probably the work of Antonio Pollaiuolo, executed shortly before his death in 1498. The floridity of the Renaissance twins clashes with the starkness of the nurturing animal.

Seeming lesions on the She-Wolf's hind legs are almost certainly traces of lightning known to have struck the Temple of Jupiter on the Capitol in 65 B.C.; the work stood there together with other sculptures that were also damaged, as Cicero reports. The sky-god who wields the thunderbolts himself authenticated Rome's totem.

The wolf, in popular perception, is more fierce and tough than noble. The shepherds and farmers who founded Rome must have known and feared the wolf packs that roamed the hillsides and the Tiber plain. Today a few wolves still live in the Abruzzi National Park southeast of the capital, and I remember an exceptionally cold winter many years ago when a lone wolf was said to have been sighted near the Colosseum. Maybe it was just a big gray stray dog.

I recall seeing and pitying the live wolves that the city used to keep in a narrow cage at the foot of the Capitoline Hill; the cruel display has long been abandoned. One of these days I'll go back to the Hall of the She-Wolf to pay my respects once again to the watchful nurturer.

• Remembrance Rites •

APRIL 25

Italy today celebrated the fiftieth anniversary of the country's complete liberation from Fascist and Nazi rule, but for most Romans this free Tuesday had meant a pillar to build a vacation "bridge" spanning from early afternoon last Friday to tomorrow morning. The most audacious bridge engineers will even stay away from their jobs until next Tuesday, because Monday, May 1, will again be a national holiday.

The principal commemoration today was held in Milan. It was there, half a century ago, that Mussolini's shrunken and shaky "Social Republic" finally collapsed, and the dictator, shot by Communist partisans at nearby Lake Como, was hanging from his heels at a service station in the Piazzale Loreto while the German divisions were surrendering to the Allied troops that had battled their way up to northern Italy from Sicily.

Freezing rain in Rome kept most people indoors, muttering what a sham the vaunted "Roman spring" was. Politicians and a few surviving veterans of the anti-Nazi resistance movement of World War II went through the remembrance rites in a wet near-void. The president of the republic, who had attended the Milan functions and flown back to the capital, laid a wreath at the Ardeatine Caves on the southern outskirts where the Gestapo had massacred 335 Italian hostages in a sinister reprisal for a bomb attack on German soldiers in 1944.

For the first time right-wingers participated in the anniversary celebrations. Among the politicians laying wreaths at the Tomb of the Unknown Soldier on the Victor Emmanuel Monument was Gianfranco Fini, leader of the party that until recently had identified itself with Il Duce's "Social Republic" and had no objection to being labeled neo-Fascist. The rightists told reporters under a downpour that the time had come for national reconciliation between former Fascists and anti-Fascists. Rome didn't seem to care.

May

• Labor Rock •

May Day, the socialist workers' festival that is a national holiday in Italy as in other European countries, nearly paralyzed Rome today. The labor unions had decreed an all-day standstill of public transport, and taxis were rare. Foreign tourists who have been crowding the city since before Easter walked a great deal, baffled and angered to find most museums, the Roman Forum, and many other sights closed.

St. Peter's was open and thronged with visitors, but the Vatican collections were inaccessible because May 1 is also a Roman Catholic feast day, dedicated to Saint Joseph the Workman.

In the city center many restaurants and espresso bars were shuttered. My American friend Jean, who lives near the Colosseum with her Italian boyfriend, wailed over the phone: "All these holidays and *ponti* [long weekends] have made me stir-crazy." She said she would walk to the Piazza San Giovanni in the late afternoon to "see people" at a rock concert in front of the Lateran Basilica.

She did see quite a few of them, at least 200,000, and so did I when I arrived there in the evening; I couldn't spot Jean. The concert was sponsored by the labor unions, and it had attracted many thousands from all over Italy, especially from the south, who had reached the capital by train or coach. Few in the vast square were over thirty.

Youngsters waved red flags with the portrait of Che Guevara; a rock group from Piedmont that was announced over the public address system as "Yo Yo Mundi" chanted a militant labor hymn, "Strike!" and an ensemble from Bari in the deep south that was said to include Greeks and Palestinians sang two Arab numbers, "Gaza" and "Intifada." Among the many other performers were a Native American, British rock stars, and Italian show personalities; the left-wing May Day music marathon was nationally televised. Plenty of police were around, but they had little to do and appeared to enjoy the songs and the atmosphere. When the mayor of Rome showed up he got tepid cheers.

• Rogue Cops •

MAY 12

Last night I came back from a brief trip to New York and Milan. Arriving by train—I was unable to get on a Milan-Rome flight—at Termini Station, I found the capital almost on its knees in a cloudburst, and I was told it had been raining hard most of the day. Buses, trams, and the subway hadn't been running since the morning because of a transit strike, scheduled for the busiest hours of the day. Many people had stayed away from their jobs for fear of being stranded.

Maybe three hundred travelers, among them many stymied foreign tourists, were lining up under the marquee at the front of the railroad terminal, waiting for cabs. There was no dispatcher, and people quarreled over the few taxis, some finally agreeing to share rides. Gypsy cabs were swarming all over the terminal, but I shunned them; instead I walked a few city blocks, carrying my bags, and found a cabbie who would take me to the Trionfale section.

I took the front seat next to him, Australian style, and he told me that he had the eight P.M. to two A.M. shift that night, and that it would be three A.M. by the time he got to his home, in the Tuscolano district near Frascati. We were repeatedly stuck in chaotic traffic. Most motorists seemed to have decided that traffic lights and other regulations were irrelevant during a transit strike. The only police officers I saw were in a squad car with its siren screaming and lights flashing that was also held up in a jumble of vehicles in the Piazzale Flaminio.

This morning the newspapers announced that many members of the municipal police were under investigation for alleged corruption and other misdeeds. I rubbed my eyes. Hadn't I read just three days earlier in New York that a number of New York City Police Department officers in the Bronx had been arrested—in fact, about 10 percent of the borough's entire police force? An Italian saying, *Tutto il mondo è paese,* came to mind; in the present context it could be freely translated as "Things are rotten everywhere."

The city police in their dark winter uniforms and their smart summer whites are the most unpopular branch of the several law enforcement organizations that look after us in Rome—often in competitive or outright antagonistic ways. For one, it is the municipal cops who write the traffic tickets. They also check up on stores and other businesses, are supposed to maintain order in the ever-crowded markets, and are involved in the building permit process. Romans I know have confessed to inducing a city policeman to tear up a traffic ticket for a price or to ignore a double-parked car.

In past years various municipal police officers were in trouble for allegedly taking bribes from business owners or contractors. In such cases City Hall usually spoke of a few "rotten apples" in its barrel of mostly sound guardians of the law.

Now all 260 officers of the municipal police's Ninth Detachment are to be interrogated by magistrates; it seems there is a lot of spoilage in that particular barrel. The detachment has jurisdiction over Rome's congested southern thoroughfare, Via Appia Nuova, as well as over the many businesses on and near it. The current affair came into the open when City Hall tried—apparently alerted by anonymous complaints—to transfer many officers of the Ninth to other districts.

The police unions protested vehemently, and the personnel of the Ninth Detachment staged several strikes. Suspicions deepened that cozy relationships between officers of the detachment, business operators, and shady local personages had long been established, and that a shuffle of personnel would tear into a web of such illegal ties. According to the local press, some municipal cops are facing allegations of blackmail; others are said to be mixed up in loan-sharking, pimping, and the flourishing drug trade.

In a City Hall press conference, Deputy Mayor Walter Tocci spoke of a "very serious situation suggesting the existence of conspiracies; crimes involving bribery and usury cannot be ruled out." The deputy mayor said the city government was putting its trust in the judiciary, and urged private citizens to report wrongdoings by the police.

• Rococo Shortcut •

MAY 15

For the first time in living memory the Spanish Staircase has been closed. Steel barriers in the Spanish Square below and in front of the Church of Trinità dei Monti at its top shut the landmark off and are to stay in place for at least eight months while the monument undergoes a thorough overhaul.

Business operators in the surrounding high-rent area are voicing outrage that the city is starting the restoration project just as the tourist season begins in earnest. I suspect City Hall has deliberately and wisely chosen the warm months for closing the Spanish Stairs to prevent further damage by the traditional hordes of summer visitors who would camp out on them.

Lately, when climbing the 137 steps of the Spanish Staircase as many Romans do every day, I have had to pick my way through people and their sprawled-out belongings. The noble sweep of mellow travertine was disfigured by graffiti and litter; chunks of the soft, porous stone that probably came from quarries near Tivoli had been broken off the steps and balustrades.

The 270-year-old rococo staircase is not only one of Rome's most beloved sight-seeing attractions, it is also an important passageway, a pedestrians' shortcut between the city's downtown core and the *quartieri alti* (high quarters) with their hotels, restaurants, embassies, banks, stores, and posh residential sections. If you want to walk from the Spanish Square to the Via Veneto or vice versa, the shortest way is now over the steep Via di San Sebastianello (which cars negotiate only in low gear) two blocks to the north, or by the narrow and equally steep stairway from the Piazza Mignanelli behind the American Express office, one block to the south.

While there is much grumbling about the interruption of a classic Roman itinerary, comic relief is provided by a row over a couple of mobile toilets (not unlike the squabble caused by similar facilities in the main square of a fictional French provincial town in Gabriel Chevallier's novel *Clochemerle*). The contracting firm that was awarded the restoration of the Spanish Stairs figured that its workers had better find toilets on the spot, otherwise they might goof off for half an hour or so every now and then. A few days before the Spanish Staircase was closed, a truck brought two wooden booths containing installations similar to those in the restrooms of aircraft. The unsightly structures were put smack in front of the Church of Trinità dei Monti, a few steps left of the five-star Hassler Hotel.

At once City Hall received dozens of irate phone calls from all over the neighborhood: "Have these eyesores removed immediately!" Local newspapers published pictures showing the toilets marring the sight of the elegant church facade adjoining its austere former convent, now an expensive private girls' school. The booths were quickly transferred to a more secluded corner at some distance from the church, the school, the hotel, and the Spanish Steps.

• Dissonances •

MAY 18

The capacity audience in the sober hall on the Via della Conciliazione were on their feet for a full ten minutes of applause and cheering when the visiting orchestra, choir, and soloists of La Scala Opera House in Milan had concluded their rendition of Verdi's *Requiem*. The president of the republic went to the podium to shake hands with the conductor, Riccardo Muti. The enthusiasm had polemical overtones. Militant unions of the Rome Opera personnel had attempted to force cancellation of the long-scheduled concert.

The orchestra and choir of La Scala hadn't performed in the capital for forty years, and Muti, the musical director of the Milan institution, had not conducted here since leading a concert in the Vatican in 1986. Renowned orchestras and maestros shun Rome because it lacks a satisfactory concert hall for classical music.

The former Augusteo, which old-timers say had good acoustics, was one of a group of buildings on the east bank of the Tiber torn down in the 1930s to bring to light the ruins of Emperor Augustus's tomb. The Augusteo, which had 3,500 seats, was a nineteenth-century structure sitting on the remains of the big circular imperial mausoleum that Emperor Augustus had built for himself and his family. The complex was often looted in later centuries, and in the Middle Ages it served as a fortress for feuding Roman baronial clans.

Deprived of an adequate concert hall, Rome has long had a low-key musical life. The orchestra of the Academy of Santa Cecilia, the principal classical music ensemble here, has for many years performed periodically in the hall of the Vatican-owned modern building on the Via della Conciliazione near St. Peter's; despite repeated attempts at improvement, the acoustics there are far from ideal.

After long debates and preparations, plans for a big new concert hall and other musical facilities are now ready at last. The Genoese architect Renzo Piano, who built the Kansai Airport off

Osaka, Japan, and important structures from Paris to Houston, won the competition for the Rome project. He envisions a shell-shaped symphony hall with 2,700 seats and two smaller halls seating twelve hundred and five hundred persons respectively; the three separate buildings are to be linked by a sweeping outdoor staircase that would accommodate thousands of listeners at open-air pop and rock events to be held in an arena below. The complex—complete with a music library, recording studios, restaurants, and parking lots for 2,500 cars—is to occupy a city-owned area on the east bank of the Tiber near the ancient Milvian Bridge in Rome's north.

If work starts this coming fall, as promised, the new concert hall could be inaugurated two years later—just in time for the reelection campaign of the present mayor and city government. It is hoped that Claudio Abbado, Italy's other world-class conductor and Muti's perennial rival, could be won for the dedication concert.

Maestro Muti and his Milan orchestra and singers were originally supposed to perform Verdi's *Requiem* in the Rome Opera House. However, labor conflicts foiled the plan. The euphoria caused by the success of *Benvenuto Cellini* in January didn't last long; the Teatro dell'Opera has produced more dissonance than harmony for the last few months. The seven unions representing musicians, singers, stagehands, and other personnel demand the rehiring of laid-off employees, promotions, and salary raises. Several scheduled performances had to be canceled on short notice, and the premiere of a new production of Léo Delibes's ballet *Coppélia* was postponed twice.

Then the unions called another strike for the day when the Teatro dell'Opera was to host the Milan orchestra under Maestro Muti. This was the final straw for Rome's mayor, who wields jurisdiction over the city's opera house. He angrily called off the proposed outdoor operatic season in the coming summer because, he said, the unions were quarrelsome and unreliable. The mayor also persuaded Muti to conduct the Milan orchestra in the hall on the Via della Conciliazione instead of in the opera house. The maestro had on earlier occasions refused to consider performances there because he didn't like how orchestral music sounded in it; this time, piqued by the inhospitable attitude of the capital's operatic unions, he relented.

Mayor Rutelli was elected with backing by his own Green movement and by left-wing groups. He has frequently made pro-labor gestures, but now he openly showed his disgust with the operatic workers. He has even threatened during the last few days to shut down the ungovernable opera house altogether. Despite the present rumble of war drums, old City Hall hands are pretty sure some sort of armistice will be negotiated just in time to do summer opera after all.

• Beer Surprise •

MAY 22

Much of the social life in this gossipy city takes place in trattorias and cafés, possibly alfresco. When a Neapolitan friend of mine, Adriano, came to town yesterday on one of his infrequent visits, I didn't invite him to my home; he didn't expect that, and I have never set foot in his place in Naples either. Instead we agreed to meet at the old birreria on the rectangular Piazza dei Santi Apostoli that he likes. Before World War I it was the place in Rome to drink Pilsen beer from Bohemia. When I first knew it, the place was called Dreher, the name of an old brewery in Trieste whose main Roman outlet it then was. The beerhouse's premises are in fact a part of the huge complex of the Palazzo Colonna. Members of the Colonna family still inhabit apartments in it.

Along with a steady Italian clientele, the old establishment used to attract Germans, Austrians, Czechs, Hungarians, and other people from central Europe living in or visiting Rome (quite a few members of the clergy among them). Over the decades I have been in the beerhouse no more than five or six times, always dragged there by other people.

Last night we were sitting at an outside table on the broad sidewalk. I found that portable trellises with creeping plants formed partitions that I didn't remember from my last visit years earlier, and that a new section with delicate white café chairs had been added. The cavernous interior looked unchanged; it might belong to one of those taverns in Trieste called "buffets."

The laminated menus showed that traditional northern Italian and central European food was still being offered. *Schnitzel* was spelled "snizzer," and there were several kinds of sausages to choose from. My friend Adriano had lasagne and beer (many southerners love beer); I ordered pizza, which turned out to be crisp and strewn with arugula (the current food fashion), and which was so large that the outsize plate beneath it disappeared. The red house wine in a quarter-liter carafe was agreeably tart and better than I had anticipated.

We were early (Adriano wanted to return to Naples the same night), and the waiter and waitress who had served us didn't yet have much to do. They were standing around on the sidewalk outside the terrace, chatting with a cute little Chinese girl. When I got the check, the heading of the computer-printed fiscal receipt read *Birreria SS. Apostoli di Wang Tse Hou & C.* The old Triestene beerhouse was now Chinese-controlled.

Like many other European cities, Rome too has witnessed a proliferation of Chinese restaurants on its soil since the 1970s. By now there are more than four hundred here, and yet another few seem to be opening in some part of the city every week. Only a handful of them are any good, a Chinese priest informed me recently. He couldn't or wouldn't answer the question Romans always ask: How do all those Chinese eating places manage to survive? Several in my own neighborhood are often empty or nearly empty at mealtimes; a score across the city were raided by police last week on suspicion of harboring illegal immigrants.

Rome has no Chinatown, not yet at any rate, although Asian faces in the streets, in the subway, and on buses have become increasingly frequent. Romans tend to call Chinese, Japanese, Filipinos, Vietnamese, and Indonesians indiscriminately *cinesi* (Chinese). But are the real or presumed Chinese in the Italian capital sufficient to assure business for all the Paper Moons, Shanghais (also spelled *Sciangai*), Shangri-las, and similarly named places? Nor can I detect any local craze for Chinese cuisine. Food is one of the few topics (soccer and sex are others) that prompt Italians to chauvinistic claims. Romans, together with their countrymen from the Alps to Sicily, will insist that the Italian cuisine is the best and healthiest in the world, a view that many other people, myself included, gladly share. When traveling abroad, Italians will always look for that insiders' place, run by an expatriate from Naples or Venice, where they will find home-style pasta al dente and real espresso, and all too often will be disappointed.

Many attempts at transplanting foreign food tastes, eating habits, and cooking fashions to this ancient city have failed; nouvelle cuisine is one example. Even posh French-inspired places that for some time experimented here with dainty hors d'oeuvres *variés* or potage as first course soon reverted to robust pasta dishes.

Hamburgers and coke, however, have won their following among young Romans.

The venerable beerhouse on the Piazza dei Santi Apostoli hasn't, for that matter, become a Chinese restaurant, although its management may be. No exotic item was on its menu, and the waiters were all Italian.

The new owners of old Dreher's, at any rate, have become tenants of a princely Roman house with a history going back to the early Middle Ages, long before Marco Polo set out from Venice to the court of the Great Khan, and according to general (though probably wrong) belief brought spaghetti back from China.

• Women in the Vatican •

MAY 25

The widow of a midlevel government official who lives in an apartment building close to ours has news about the pope: John Paul II has lately become "irritable and moody," and seems to trust only the Polish ecclesiastics in his Vatican entourage. Rumors that the pontiff is in poor health have been going around ever since he underwent surgery for a tumor and especially after he fell last year and broke a hipbone. He is just back from a two-day visit to the Czech Republic and a short trip to the Polish mountains near his birthplace, Wadowice; on television we saw that he walked, or rather shuffled, with difficulty and looked tired. Yet he promised the people of Prague he would return to the Czech Republic "in two years."

When our neighbor, the old lady, told me about the dark papal moods, I listened attentively. Why should the widow who rarely goes out and sees very few people know more about John Paul II than the newspapers care to print? The fact is that on various occasions over several years she came up with Vatican information that was eventually to prove accurate.

She learns such news from one of her daughters-in-law whose sister works in Vatican City. This connection is one of hundreds, maybe thousands, of tiny cracks in the walls of secrecy with which the pontifical state surrounds itself, and which are no less formidable than its stone ramparts that Michelangelo designed. Drop by drop quite a lot of what is going on inside seeps out. While the pope and his aides are kept minutely informed of everything happening in the city that embraces their enclave, the Romans too, by osmosis, get to know a great deal of Vatican gossip.

The sister of the widow's daughter-in-law who holds a Vatican job is no nun. She is an unmarried woman in her thirties who ten years ago was hired as a computer operator by an administrative office in the pontifical state; meanwhile she appears to have risen to a quasi-executive position under the supervision of a high prelate. She was pointed out to me a couple of years ago when, with her sister, she left after visiting the old lady who is a neighbor of ours. I remember her as a chubbily attractive, fashionably dressed blonde. Later I was told she lives in a nice apartment in a church-owned building not far from the Vatican, has a Filipina maid, and in August every year spends her vacations in Switzerland. Inevitably there is talk that she has a clerical friend.

She is one of several hundred women who work in the Vatican and its appendages around Rome along with almost four thousand men, most of whom—but by no means all—are priests and friars. Most of the Holy See's female workforce are members of religious orders, from Polish nuns doing the housekeeping for the pope to telephone operators and mother superiors serving as consultants to the central church government.

The Vatican's almost fifteen hundred lay wage earners, male and female, now have their own union. Cardinals, archbishops,

bishops, and lower clergy working in the papal state get paid too but don't belong to the union; many priests, friars, and nuns in Vatican jobs are maintained by their own religious orders and communities and cost the papal treasury nothing.

None of the laywomen in Vatican jobs have living quarters in the State of Vatican City as far as I know, but several male lay employees reside in the 108.7-acre territory with their families.

To land a Vatican job is a coveted prize in Rome. The pay is relatively low—from $750 to $1,850 a month, tax-free—but employment is presumably for one's working life; in addition, many staff members manage to maneuver at least one of their children into positions in the papal state. Vatican workers enjoy more paid holidays than do wage earners in Italy because the Holy See observes religious feasts—like Saints Peter and Paul's Day on June 29—that the Italian republic ignores.

Most important, Vatican employment entails substantial fringe benefits. Many Vatican workers live in low-rent apartments in one of the many church-owned houses throughout Rome. Fuel for one's car is cheaper at the Vatican gas pump than at any service station outside. Food and other merchandise, especially textiles, is sold at favorable prices at the Annona, a supermarket on Vatican territory. (The Latin word *annona* originally meant the annual corn harvest, and eventually denoted produce in general.) For years we used to get imported coffee and butter of the best quality from an obliging friend whose late father worked in the Vatican and shopped at Annona. The supply line was cut when our friend moved to a country house far from Rome.

Envied though the Vatican's lay employees generally are, they have to observe a strict moral code in their private lives. Divorce, cohabitation or pregnancy without marriage, or an abortion (if proved) will mean instant dismissal.

The widow who spoke about the pope's mood swings gets occasional provisions from the Vatican Annona by way of her daughter-in-law; it's probably mostly coffee—she is very thin and seems to live mainly on cappuccino. Whenever I run into her, which is seldom enough, I never question her about her tenuous but informative Vatican connection; we always talk about her late husband, whom I knew and esteemed, and about her sons, who appear to be doing well in life. It is the widow who volunteers the papal news.

This morning a former colleague, an Italian journalist specializing in Vatican news—a *vaticanista*—whom I have known for decades, confirmed the old lady's information. I met him by chance when I was looking for a pay phone in the Borgo Vittorio, a picturesque old street near Vatican City, and found the nearest one in an espresso bar and tavern where off-duty members of the papal Swiss Guard hang out. After the phone call I asked the counterman to filter me an espresso, and found myself side by side with my ex-colleague, who was sipping an aperitivo at the bar.

He is a veteran. We were on the same plane with Pope Paul VI when he visited Australia and Oceania in 1970. I hadn't seen the *vaticanista* for several years, and of course asked him how he was doing on his beat.

He told me that he and the other *vaticanisti*, prodded by their editors, were all bringing up to date the biographies of potential successors to the papal throne. "The sovereign"—my former colleague always used to refer to the pope that way—"has his ups and downs. He is often short-tempered with his aides, which is a new thing. He probably is in pain; we are convinced that his hip surgery wasn't a full success. Any idea, is there an American candidate for succession to the sovereign?"

• Horse Ballet •

MAY 28

The Sixty-third International Horse Show of Rome ended tonight, bathed in floodlights, as 145 mounted Carabinieri in their gala uniforms and high red-and-blue tufted hats performed their carousel. This year's bravura horse ballet number and the riding and jumping contests of the last four days, organized by the Equine Sports Federation and sponsored by big business groups, were part of a television spectacular rather than the culminating event of the Roman high-society season that they once used to be.

In truth, the horse show in the Piazza di Siena, the pine-girded oval square in the Villa Borghese gardens, was never an Italian Epsom. No gray high hats or other Derby attire were ever worn there, and no Indian potentate would attend. Yet the Roman nobility once imitated the horsy rituals of the British upper crust in other ways. During my very first years in this city a few snobbish counts and princes would still don red coats a couple of mornings in the fall, assemble on the Via Cassia on the city's far northern outskirts, and ride to hounds, harrying a luckless fox that somehow had been procured and let loose in the no-longer-so-lonely Roman campagna.

After the pathetic foxhunts became a fading memory, Roman palazzi would still open for parties during the annual Horse Show. Earlier in the day, Roman aristocrats and foreign ambassadors would have stoically sat through the horse-jumping competitions in the Piazza di Siena, braving the drizzles and occasional downpours that seemed part of the program.

I spotted very few members of the Roman nobility or the diplomatic corps in the grandstand this year, but, blessedly, it didn't rain either. The organizers at last had moved the Horse Show a month from its traditional date, the end of April, to the last week in May. The fact is that April and much of May are rarely favored by the weather gods here. This city enjoys long, glorious autumns, but "Roman spring" is fictional. We are more likely to bask in tepid sunshine on pleasant days in February and March.

On the opening afternoon of the Horse Show last Wednesday, when the late-afternoon sun was still strong, I overheard some women in garden hats and summer dresses comment that "This year we haven't had any spring. First, chilly weather and rain for weeks, and then, bang! summer is here and it's getting hot." I hear this remark dozens of times every year, always uttered in a tone suggesting that an extraordinary meteorological phenomenon has been observed. Actually, a rainy spring and the brusque start of a long, hot summer is the normal sequence in the Roman year.

In the grandstand quite a few men were in shirtsleeves during the last few days. Some ticket holders sneaked from their seats to the sidelines for picnics on the grass in the Glyndebourne Festival manner as soon as the main contests were over and the binoculars could be put to rest.

Sixty-eight riders from ten nations competed, and foreigners— French and German champions in particular—won most events. The Japanese team of beautiful horses bought from European breeders showed much progress in comparison with earlier appearances here—at least that's what an Italian military officer who seemed to be a Piazza di Siena habitué condescendingly said in a loud voice.

I watched on television some of the Horse Show events that took place later this week. The red and deep blue coats, white trousers, black boots, and dark caps of the riders, the magnificently groomed horses, and the green lawn and pine trees created a gorgeous picture. The camera never failed to pan on female riders' backsides as they rhythmically lifted from their saddles. Leave it to Roman video crews!

• Lunch Protest •

MAY 30

Two tables covered with red-checkered tablecloths holding bowls of a Neapolitan-style pasta called fusilli and bottles of mineral water stood on the sidewalk outside the Treasury Ministry in the Via Venti Settembre at lunchtime today. Hundreds of government workers milling around outside the building ate heaping portions of the pasta from disposable plates and drank water from paper cups.

"The fusilli are almost cold and overcooked, and there's no wine," a man in suit and tie, who looked like a subaltern bureaucrat, complained disgustedly. "I hate having lunch standing up like a horse," he added.

There was no wine, but there were plenty of civil service union banners, and signs reading "Attention—Workers' Time Out for the Ministerial Lunch Break" and "More Duties and Fewer Rights— Europe, Italian Style!"

The frugal sidewalk lunch was one of organized labor's current protests against a change in the working hours of government employees aimed at bringing them into line with those in other countries of the European Union. The new "European" schedules affect the lives of a sizable segment of this city's population.

For seven decades, government workers in Rome have been enjoying free afternoons, or overtime pay if they were ordered to be at their jobs after their late lunches. The system, known as "unbroken schedule," was introduced by Mussolini as a privilege for the legions of state employees in the nation's capital. They were supposed to work continuously from eight A.M. to two P.M., Monday to Saturday.

Now the government wants its offices in Rome, as in the rest of the country, to be normally staffed also in the afternoon, at least until 3:45, Monday to Friday, and most of the personnel will be free Saturday and Sunday. The new work schedule is called the "short week," and lunch breaks, to be taken in turns, are not to last longer than half an hour.

While the reform is officially motivated with adherence to "European" standards, it is also being enacted to save the Treasury huge funds previously swallowed by overtime payments. Not surprisingly, almost all government workers in Rome, especially women, are angrily opposed to the "short week." For one thing, thousands of female state employees now face unexpected household and child care problems. A national television network last night showed a woman walking out of a government building, indignantly tossing her head and hissing to a reporter that her new job schedule was "crazy."

Romans who don't hold government jobs seem rather pleased. The conviction is widespread here that public employees don't work very hard. For one thing, the eight A.M. start of their working day has long been theoretical. If attendance in government offices was taken at all, it was done around nine A.M. after all employees with small children had taken them to school, done other chores, and found parking spaces near their offices.

After ten A.M., government offices start emptying again. Scores of times over the years I tried to reach some functionary around midmorning, only to be told that *il dottore* or *la dottoressa* was in a meeting and couldn't be called to the telephone. The meeting, nine times out of ten, was taking place in an espresso bar in the building or at a nearby street corner outside, and what was discussed with colleagues was the soccer championship or the latest twist in a favorite soap opera.

The unofficial midmorning break not only was a chance for gossip but also had a physiological reason. Most Romans take very little for breakfast, often just a cup of espresso on the run, and crave a cappuccino and a plump *cornetto*, the ubiquitous croissant, between ten and eleven A.M. to keep going until their delayed lunch.

I have known government employees, male and female alike, who managed to spin out their cappuccino pause into hour-long shopping expeditions in the neighborhood. Plenty of merchandise is available on government premises. Some of the in-house espresso bars and cafeterias stock everything from pantyhose to encyclopedias, and I have heard of employees who sell lingerie or perfumes, taken on commission, to colleagues during office hours.

As for the end of the bureaucratic working day, I have personally watched at the Ministry of Industry, Commerce, and Handicrafts in the Via Veneto how scores of office workers gather near the rear exit as early as 1:30 P.M., anxious to be the first out of the building when the doors open. At two P.M. sharp the ministerial personnel would stream into the street like kids let out of school.

Generations of new-broom cabinet ministers have striven in vain to keep their staffs available to superiors and the public during office hours. Time clocks and attendance lists didn't help much; if you were late or needed an hour off for some private business, there was always a colleague who would cover for you; next time you would reciprocate. Some department chiefs, bowing to the inevitable, ruled that one cappuccino break during the "unbroken" schedule was okay, but it mustn't take longer than twenty minutes.

Now, with the introduction of the "short week," department heads again issue the usual service circulars, warning staffs that work schedules must be painstakingly observed and that strict controls would make sure that they were. Romans must have heard similar edicts in antiquity.

It may be safely predicted that the cappuccino ritual will continue as before, and that the midday break will gradually expand from half an hour to at least an hour—no Roman lunch lasts less. Wait until summer with its heat and siesta drowsiness is here! In a city that virtually closes down between one and four or five P.M., with all stores shuttered and people either taking a nap or hankering for one, you can't expect government workers alone to suddenly be alert and keen.

June

• Border Conflict •

While we were asleep, our neighborhood was the scene of an international conflict with an attempt at hostage taking; I missed the excitement, learning of it only late this morning. Nearly a dozen men of the Pontifical Swiss Guard were said to have clashed with Italian police last night.

The incident, pitting security forces of two sovereign states against each other, started a few blocks from where I live. The

Switzers, all lanky fellows in their late twenties sporting civilian dress, were off duty and apparently unarmed. They had been watching a thrilling game of the Swiss soccer championship on satellite television in a tavern—Grasshoppers Zurich versus a team from the city of Sion in the Valais. They also seem to have had a lot to drink.

By one A.M. the guardsmen found it was time to return to their billets in the nearby Vatican. Fired by the wine and soccer enthusiasm, they sang and yelled as they marched across the Prati section. Its long, straight streets, laid out at the turn of the century, are usually quiet and full of parked cars at that hour of the night. The guttural Swiss sounds no doubt awakened quite a few people living there. Two civilians, one of them a lawyer, who had had a long evening and were returning home noticed that the exuberant Swiss were vandalizing parked autos; the lawyer called the police emergency number, 113, from a pay telephone and reported what was happening.

Minutes later two patrol cars of the state police arrived at the indicated spot in the Via dei Gracchi, but the noisy troop had meanwhile marched on. The police quickly caught up with the frisky Swiss near the Piazza Risorgimento, close to the Vatican walls, where it seems they had also kicked dents into cars. The guardsmen were finally confronted outside the Gate of Saint Anne, one of the three major entrances to Vatican City, where they were waiting for the door to open. The ten P.M. curfew for priests and laypeople living in the papal state does not apply to off-duty members of the Swiss Guard.

After a brief scuffle, the Italians managed to handcuff two Swiss, but the remaining Swiss squeezed through the electronic gate and tried to drag one of the Italians with them onto Vatican territory. The idea was apparently to use the policeman as a hostage to be traded for the handcuffed guardsmen.

The supposed hostage, however, succeeded in wresting himself free and regaining Italian soil as the gate clanked shut. The escaped guardists entered their barracks and presumably reported their version of what had happened to a superior. The squad cars with their prisoners drove to the nearest police station. The two detained Swiss were booked for malicious mischief and assault, and were told they would have to spend the night in a holding cell. Then diplomacy took over.

After an exchange of late-night telephone calls between dignitaries of the Holy See and high Italian officials, the deputy commander of the Pontifical Swiss Guard turned up at the police station, offered an apology, and took the two men with him to the Vatican.

The pope was in all likeliness informed early this morning of the frontier incident at the gate that separates the state of Vatican City from the Italian republic. John Paul II must have been annoyed—the Polish pontiff, as bishop of Rome, is known to attach much importance to good relations with the Italian authorities. Even if Italy doesn't press charges against the implicated guardsmen, they will probably be disciplined in the Vatican and perhaps sent home.

It seems no sergeant or commissioned officer of the Swiss Guard was in the fight with the Italian police, just halberdiers. The privates of the papal army actually carry halberds when they don their blue-, red-, and yellow-striped Renaissance-style uniforms, which, according to contradictory accounts, were designed by either Raphael or Michelangelo. The Switzers, who present their halberds to the pontiff, high churchmen, and state visitors, are actually well-trained soldiers who have done their compulsory military service in the Swiss army before enlisting in the Vatican force. Their equipment in the papal service also includes firearms, and they have periodic shooting practice at an Italian rifle range on Rome's northern outskirts.

Last night's fracas came only four weeks after the Swiss Guard commemorated the anniversary of the corps' heroism during the Sack of Rome in A.D. 1527. On May 6 of that year, when the invading soldiery of Emperor Charles V terrorized the city, 147 of the Vatican's 189 Swiss mercenaries died to save the life of Pope Clement VII.

At present the Swiss Guard has a strength of fewer than a hundred halberdiers and officers. Former guardsmen keep in touch. A friend of mine in Lucerne, now in a municipal job after years in papal service, told me recently: "We Guard veterans meet every year in some place in Switzerland or abroad. We'll never forget our time in Rome." Ah, those off-duty hours beyond the Gate of Saint Anne!

• Graduate with a Broom •

JUNE 8

Our neighborhood got a new street-cleaning squad and now looks tidier, at least in the early afternoon, than it has in years. We have a big outdoor market in the Trionfale section and, a few blocks closer to where I live, the city's wholesale flower market. Empty cartons that held tulips from the Netherlands or orchids from Thailand litter our sidewalks in the morning. Once known as "the Garden of Europe," Italy now imports lots of flowers, and some dealers just fling the packaging into the street. By two P.M. on most days, however, our sidewalks are neat, and the green Dumpsters into which householders put their garbage are emptied.

Today when I saw three green-uniformed "ecological operators" (as garbage collectors are now correctly called), I stopped to chat. They were two women and a strapping man, maybe in his late twenties. They had just finished pouring the contents of the

Dumpsters into the maw of a churning garbage-compressor truck, had taken off their heavy-duty gloves, and had marched into the espresso bar at the street corner for a cappuccino before sweeping the sidewalks with the brooms they had leaned against the outer wall.

"Are you the *ingegnere?*" I asked the male of the team. He grinned and nodded. Neighbors had told me of him. In Rome a polytechnic graduate is addressed as *ingegnere* (engineer), a title more prestigious than *dottore* (doctor). An *ingegnere* is regarded as someone more solid and serious than a mere doctor, who by no means has to be a physician but may be a graduate from law school or may have studied letters or business administration, or is just a dropout who is called *dottore* anyway because of wearing eyeglasses.

The *ingegnere* in his green overalls guessed my unexpressed question. "Why have I taken this job?" he said. "For two years I couldn't find anything else, and I have a wife and a little girl. When I applied for this, I didn't tell them of my degree. Let's hope something different comes up later." He indicated the younger of his two female colleagues: "This signorina should teach school, but there aren't enough children in Italy today."

I told the trio that neighborhood people were full of praise for their work. "The Romans ought to be less messy!" the older of the two women, who appeared to be the leader of the cleaning detail, said tartly. "People throw things on the pavement even if a garbage can is only two meters distant; they don't care. And let's not talk about the dogs!"

The schoolteacher without kids to teach remarked: "It's not just the Romans. I have worked near the Vatican for a few weeks, and you wouldn't believe what the tourists do! Plastic bottles, half-eaten sandwiches, gelato cones—everything ends up on the pavement. Then they return home and say the Romans are dirty."

• Quake Scare •

JUNE 13

Most Roman families were at dinner or watching the evening news—or both—when the ground below us shuddered. Some clocks stopped at 8:13 P.M. The floor lamp near which I was reading swayed and might have toppled if I hadn't steadied it. Burglar alarms, set off by the earthquake, were wailing all around. The tremor lasted barely three seconds, the radio would announce in a news flash an hour later, but the glasses in our cupboard tinkled for minutes, and the chandelier kept swinging much longer.

I went around the apartment and inspected the landing and staircase to see if there were any cracks or other damage; to my relief I saw none. Then I did what a lot of other people did: I worked the phone, contributing to a network overload. Calling friends around the city, I found, whenever I could get through to them, that the quake had been felt in some neighborhoods much more strongly than in ours.

Emma, a friend of my wife's who lives in the Monteverde section on the southwestern outskirts, reported she was watering her flowers on the balcony when the parapet started to shake and she was afraid she would plunge with it into the street below. Patches of masonry had come off in her kitchen, and a tiled bathroom wall had split.

We soon learned that the tremor had been most violent in the modern districts on the far south of the city with their housing projects and high-rises—some of them flimsily built. Thousands had rushed into the open. Many had slammed their doors on fleeing their apartments, forgetting to take their keys with them, and would later need assistance from the fire department to get back into their homes. Quite a few people spent the night in their cars for fear of more and stronger tremors.

By ten P.M., broadcasts informed us that the epicenter of the quake had been near Ardea, an ancient town close to the seashore fifteen miles south of Rome, and that the seismic event was thought to have occurred six miles below the surface. It was rated at 6 on the Mercalli scale (3.9 on the more widely used Richter scale). Italians cling to the twelve-step scale for measuring the intensity of earthquakes proposed by the seismologist Giuseppe Mercalli in the early twentieth century.

Nobody appeared to have been hurt, and no building had to be evacuated. The authorities stated there was no reason for fearing that a major earthquake was imminent (how did they know?) and urged people to stay in their homes to foil "jackals" (looters).

A cluster of minor tremors came during the night and this morning, as seismologists expected. The president of the National Institute of Geophysics, Enzo Boschi, noted that yesterday's tremor seemed an "almost perfect replica" of one that had occurred a hundred years earlier. Only, there was much less fright then, he remarked, because Rome was much smaller, and the area principally affected by the quake was still rural and thinly inhabited.

The deputy president of the geophysics institute, Renato Funiciello, stated records showed that Rome had experienced 655 earth shocks between 461 B.C. and a strong one in 1989 that had its epicenter in the Alban Hills southeast of the city. Those hills, he said, were spent volcanoes that had been active until "only" thirty thousand years ago.

The Colosseum and other Roman landmarks suffered heavy damages in a number of seismic disasters in the Middle Ages and again in 1703. In a catastrophic earthquake on January 13, 1915, some thirty thousand persons died in the Abruzzi Mountains east of the capital, and more than fifty churches in Rome's center were damaged.

• Cross and Crescent •

JUNE 21

The first day of summer brought the first genuine seasonal heat, and the sun was as powerful in Rome as it is in the Arabian desert. Appropriately, the first mosque in the city of the popes was solemnly inaugurated on the northern outskirts. Young palm trees had been planted around the new complex, but their leaves hardly moved in the absence of any noticeable breeze, and shade was scarce. Dark eyeglasses did little to soften the glare of the marble and travertine structures—a circular prayer hall for two thousand worshipers with its bluish dome; a minaret; and an Islamic center with a Koran school and a library.

While the Italian notables in dark suits and a handful of Roman Catholic churchmen in their black cassocks appeared uncomfortable in the midday swelter, the Arab dignitaries who had come for the ceremony appeared quite at ease. They were led by the towering emir of Riad, Prince Salman ibn Abdul Aziz al-Saud, in a black cape, representing his brother, King Fahd. Saudi Arabia had paid $35 million of the $50 million that the mosque project had cost, while twenty-two other Islamic states shared the remainder of the expense.

Unofficially the mosque has been functioning for more than a year as a religious center, a meeting place, and a market for Rome's Muslims. How many of them are there? For years I have been hearing fifty thousand, although the local authorities say they know of only 38,000. Actually there may be many more than fifty thousand because of the continued influx of illegal immigrants from Africa, the Middle East, Pakistan, Albania, and Bosnia.

Thousands, at any rate, attended prayers at the new mosque during Ramadan earlier this year. As long ago as the late 1980s, City Hall changed the name of the winding street skirting the Islamic compound from Viale di Forte Antenne into Viale della Moschea (Mosque Avenue) and stepped up service of the No. 230 bus line on Fridays to enable the faithful to reach the mosque more easily.

A few restaurants serving couscous and other North African and Middle Eastern dishes have sprung up in the neighborhood lately, and halal butchers sell meat from ritually slaughtered animals; hawkers peddle merchandise, such as strings of beads, in the mosque area on Fridays.

The idea of a Muslim presence in the holy city of Roman Catholic Christianity was first advanced by King Faisal of Saudi Arabia in talks with Italian government leaders in the early 1970s. Influential Roman Catholic churchmen weren't too pleased, but Pope Paul VI and his two successors had no objections, especially after assurances were received that no minaret would compete with the dome of St. Peter's on the city's skyline because the proposed mosque would be tucked away on an outlying site.

For that purpose the city government donated a 7.5-acre area at the foot of the Monte Antenne, a two-hundred-foot hill between the Tiber and the Via Salaria, the national highway that follows the ancient "salt road" to the Adriatic Sea. Monte Antenne isn't named after broadcasting antennas—as many Romans believe—but after a Sabine village, Antemnae, that 2,500 years ago sat on the hill; Antemnae was said to have been one of the targets of ancient Roman raiders who pulled off the legendary abduction of the Sabine women.

Early Christian catacombs pierce the subsoil along the Via Salaria, as they do in the vicinity of other Roman roads. For many centuries the site was abandoned to shepherds and their flocks. Aristocrats cut themselves vast chunks of land for country mansions and parks. One of those properties, known as the Villa Ada, became the private residence of the Italian royal family, the Savoys, after Rome assumed the role as capital of the unified nation. Now a public park, the former royal estate adjoins the Monte Antenne where military engineers built a little fort in the late nineteenth century, one of a string of fortifications around Rome that were to defend the capital from possible attacks but proved totally useless.

A team of two Italian architects, Paolo Portoghesi and Vittorio Gigliotti, won a competition for the mosque project; an Iraqi colleague, Sami Mousawi, served as Muslim adviser.

Red tape and disagreements between the Muslim sponsors of the undertaking and local authorities and lobbies caused long delays. One major point of contention was the proposed minaret. The original designs foresaw a height of 262 feet, but neighborhood people and environmentalists protested, and the tower was scaled down to one hundred feet. The residential district, Parioli, around Monte Antenne and south of it was developed after World War I and especially during the Fascist dictatorship as an upper-class section with elegant villas and condominiums.

Parioli today is no longer quite as exclusive as it was in the neighborhood's early years, but it's still considered swank. Inhabitants of housing near the mosque made it clear to City Hall that they didn't care to be awakened in the morning by a muezzin's chant. They received the promise there wouldn't be any prayer calls, live or recorded, from the minaret.

Then there came the discovery that the mihrab (prayer niche) of the original designs hadn't exactly pointed toward Mecca, as it must. Back to the drawing board. Actual construction work started in 1984 and proceeded by fits and starts.

Maybe it was the sudden heat or the location on the far outskirts, but Romans today overwhelmingly seemed to ignore the
mosque's inauguration, although after all it was the rare thing—a
historic first in a city that has seen so much. Some conservatives
were known to mutter that the event marked Islam's comeback in
Europe, an epochal revenge for the Crusades. At any event, there
were no more than a few dozen curious people outside the mosque
compound, which was ringed by strong security forces while a
police helicopter cruised overhead.

The president of the republic was half an hour late for the
ceremony, which was slow in getting underway as the merciless
sun rose higher and higher. The mayor of Rome was present, as
were three former prime ministers and a few members of Parliament. The Vatican was represented by three second-string
prelates, and the Italian Jewish community, which counts 35,000
people nationwide, by its president, Tullia Zevi. Somehow a
troop of gypsies, posing as devout Muslims, had managed to
gain admission, and brazenly asked the official guests for handouts.

After lengthy official speeches in Arabic and Italian the guests
were led from the auditorium into the prayer hall for a quick look.
Visitors were allowed to keep their shoes on as a blue carpet was
covering the floor. To me the interior of the mosque seemed to be
conceived in a highly eclectic style, its twenty-eight columns
opening upward into a welter of branches. Mr. Mousawi, the Iraqi
architect, explained that the columns were meant to recall those
of the mosque in Córdoba, Spain.

The Italian media described Rome's first mosque as the "largest
in Europe," as if Istanbul with its grandiose Islamic buildings didn't
belong to the Continent.

At about the same time as the invited guests at the mosque
were at last heading for the buffet tables, Pope John Paul II

addressed thousands of participants in his weekly general audience in the Vatican. He briefly mentioned the Islamic ceremony.
It was significant, he said, that in Rome, "the center of Christendom and seat of the successor of Saint Peter," Muslims too had
now their own place of worship. Unfortunately, the pontiff added,
in "some Islamic countries similar recognition of religious liberty is
missing," voicing the hope that "at the threshold of the third millennium" such attitudes would change.

One of the churchmen at the mosque's inauguration told me
that the Vatican has a Pontifical Institute for Arabic and Islamic
Studies (which issues a polyglot magazine, *Islamochristiana*), whereas
in Saudi Arabia there isn't one Christian church, and a visiting
priest may not even say Mass privately in his hotel room.

POSTSCRIPT, JUNE 23

A group of Roman Catholic traditionalists gathered in the parish
church of Saint Luigi Gonzaga, near the mosque, last night to pray
the rosary as an "atonement" for what they said was an outrage to
the faith. They meant to denounce the opening of an Islamic center "in the city where the Apostles Saint Peter and Saint Paul were
martyred." There was a stir when the president (speaker) of the
Chamber of Deputies, Irene Pivetti, escorted by her official bodyguards, arrived in the church to do some silent praying for a quar-
ter of an hour. Miss Pivetti, a thirty-two-year-old Milanese who at
present is Italy's third-highest official (after the president of the
republic and the speaker of the Senate) is a devout, conservative
Catholic; cartoonists love to depict her as an Italian Joan of Arc.
Her office stated later she had visited the Church of Saint Luigi
Gonzaga in a private capacity, but ambassadors from Muslim
countries expressed irritation at her gesture.

• Faux Folklore •

An invitation to a party that I couldn't get out of brought me to the roof garden of the Cavalieri Hilton Hotel on top of the Monte Mario last night. Most of the people at the reception didn't know one another, there was the customary assault at the buffet, and the evening was even more boring than such official affairs usually are. The grand panorama, vaster than the view from my own terrace some 250 feet lower on the slope, revealed to me how far Rome's northern outskirts had lately expanded.

What impressed me most, even jolted me, at the Hilton occurred when I entered the hotel complex. A line of American tourists, visibly well-to-do, was waiting under the marquee at the entrance to board a fleet of taxis that were driving up one after the other. The men, all middle-aged and many of them paunchy, wore Hawaiian shirts or white dinner jackets; their women were, without exception, in long dresses.

Where do you go in Rome in such attire at eight P.M. in summer? The opera house was closed, and unless the group had been invited to some embassy garden party I couldn't imagine where they were heading. Even in a deluxe restaurant here guests wearing formal clothes (or Hawaiian shirts, for that matter) on a balmy night in late June will cause the same surprise as would a diner dressed up as Batman.

The enigma was quickly solved when I overheard the doorman give directions to one of the cabbies. He named a restaurant in the Trastevere section specializing in faux folklore for moneyed foreign tourists. Its waiters are disguised as shepherds out of an early-nineteenth-century genre painting and address every patron in

English; the band and the singers impersonate Abruzzi bandits the way Gothic novels in Jane Austen's time used to describe them. The musical offerings alternate between Neapolitan songs and international pop numbers. The noise level is so high that it drowns out any attempt at conversation, which may be a good thing if you must entertain some unsophisticated visitors and have nothing to say to them. The food and wines are mediocre.

The night on the town won't be cheap for the Hilton Hotel group, but they will probably have a great time; they may even tell the folks back home they have experienced a slice of the real Rome.

To recuperate from the hangovers that too much of the dubious wine is bound to produce, some of tonight's revelers will remain at the hotel tomorrow instead of taking part in the events scheduled for the day (ten minutes in the Sistine Chapel? A coach trip to the waterworks in Tivoli?).

The hotel compound overlooking the city from its 450-foot altitude includes a large swimming pool, tennis courts, and well-groomed gardens. Public controversy arose when the Cavalieri Hilton was about to be built soon after World War II. The environmental movement wasn't as strong then as it is today, but vocal protests were lodged against the large hotel project on the ground that it would spoil Rome's skyline. A compromise between the promoters of the hotel and the conservationists was eventually struck: the Cavalieri Hilton wasn't built as tall as originally planned. It now has 374 rooms, some of them combined into elegant suites, and is a fine cosmopolitan hotel operation. And it is about as typical of Rome and Roman life as the cricket clubs of Johannesburg and Pretoria were typical of South Africa under the apartheid system.

July

• Ailing Amphitheater •

The central government's superintendent of archeology announced today that long-overdue work to restore and consolidate the Colosseum will at last start later this month. The $25 million project is to be completed in four years, so that by the beginning of the third millennium the city's most famous landmark will be resplendent in a rejuvenated look.

That the 1,900-year-old ruined amphitheater should be regarded throughout the world as the quintessential symbol of Rome, the way the Eiffel Tower is for Paris, has always disturbed me. Whether or not lions tore Christians limb from limb in the Colosseum, its arena was the stage for brutal popular entertainment—gladiatorial fights, bloodshed, savage cruelty to humans and animals. Today's Romans may riot lustily in the soccer stadium, but they wouldn't tolerate for a minute a Colosseum show such as offered by "good" Emperor Titus to the city's lazy populace.

Apart from its sanguinary past, the Colosseum is of course also a monument to the impressive skills and technology of ancient Roman architects. The huge building has withstood wars, lightning and fires, earthquakes, and depredations. Middle Ages and Renaissance contractors used it as a convenient quarry for obtaining prehewn building blocks for the churches and palaces they were erecting.

A more insidious and continuing danger to the huge structure has been erosion by water and vegetation. Nineteenth-century botanists identified more than four hundred kinds of plants growing in the ruin. The mosses, herbs, and flowers that loosened the stones of the Colosseum were repeatedly removed, and massive early-nineteenth-century buttresses prevented endangered parts of the amphitheater from collapsing.

New threats to the Colosseum arose during the last few decades: air pollution gnawing at its travertine and tufa blocks, and vibration from the hectic surface traffic and the forty-year-old B line of the subway, whose trains rumble through a nearby tunnel. Stones from the upper tiers of the Colosseum have repeatedly crashed to the ground lately. Nobody has been hurt, fortunately, but the increasing shakiness of the old structure evidently represented a public hazard.

Adriano La Regina, whose sonorous title—Superintendent of the Archeological Patrimony of Rome—comes with awesome responsibility, has long pressed for a complete overhaul of the amphitheater. Three years ago a financial institution, the Banca di Roma, undertook to fund the restoration project, but red tape caused the usual delays. From now on, during the next four years, visitors to Rome will see the Colosseum in part trussed by steel scaffolding as one segment after another is repaired.

• Ice Shavings •

JULY 10

Scores of young people linger near the green-painted sheet-iron booth of Sora Maria on an intersection near my home from early afternoon to long after midnight, sipping her cold concoctions while gossiping and joking. Some of the customers always occupy the two or three chairs that she illegally puts on the sidewalk; others sit on their motor scooters or in a car on the curbside with its doors open; others just stand around, glass in hand, as at a cocktail party.

The clustering patrons won't move if you want to pass, so you are forced either to walk in the middle of the Via Trionfale, watching for oncoming traffic, or to cross over to the opposite sidewalk.

The booming business of Sora Maria is a sure sign that the Roman summer has arrived. _Sora_ is Roman dialect for signora; Mrs. Maria is a short, gruff-looking woman who must be in her seventies. Until last year she was gray-haired, but now she is a brunette. I don't remember ever having seen her smile in the twenty (or thirty?) summers I have been passing her stand. Maybe she smiles in winter.

During the hot season Sora Maria daily dispenses hundreds, possibly thousands, of glasses filled almost to the brim with flakes that she shaves with a scraper from a block of ice. When I was a small boy it was one of my jobs to buy a fraction of such a frozen block at a nearby beer garden and take it home for our icebox. Astonishingly, with all the state-of-the-art refrigeration systems, somebody in Rome must still produce and market such ice blocks.

From a battery of bottles on a shelf, Sora Maria pours a little colored liquid into the ice-filled glasses to the customers' specifications: lemon or orange juice, red raspberry juice, green mint syrup, and others. Romans like to drink the stuff in hot weather, watching the ice shavings slowly melt in their glass and mix with the juice. Many customers ask for seconds. Police patrol cars drive up from time to time. The officers get out, unbutton their tunics, ask for a glass with their favorite flavor, and chat up the girls who are always around Sora Maria's booth.

A female assistant, maybe a niece of Sora Maria, washes the glasses in a small hamper between servings. I have my doubts that the ice blocks and the rest of the operation would pass a strict health test, but apparently there has never been a complaint. Sora Maria, at any rate, functions as a pleasant social neighborhood center; there never has been a row there, as far as I know.

Sora Maria is a *grattachecca,* an old Roman institution. The word is composed of the verb for "to scrape," *grattare,* and the dialect noun *checca,* which in today's slang denotes a gay man, though in a more ancient meaning it was an obscenity referring to the female anatomy. There are still eight or ten licensed *grattachecche* in business in various city neighborhoods, although no longer at the center.

Neither will one spot a *cocomeraro* in Rome's historic core, although there are plenty of them in the popular outlying districts. They sell slices of chilled *cocomero,* the juicy red watermelon that is another favorite treat these days when temperatures soar to around 100 degrees Fahrenheit day after day. This season's price for a slice of watermelon is 1,000 lire, about 60¢ at the going exchange rate.

I haven't worn a necktie in weeks—I would look weird if I did. Almost all the people I see, even in the elegant shopping streets of the center, are dressed as if the city were a sea resort, and in a way it is—an appendage to the popular beaches of nearby Ostia and the higher-class Fregene. Several people I know have taken summer houses on the seacoast and commute to their jobs in Rome.

Only the Vatican for some reason has suddenly tightened its dress code. Papal security men at the entrance to St. Peter's inexorably keep out women in miniskirts or with bare shoulders and men wearing shorts or athletic shirts. Tight trousers for women that reveal their shapes are all right, but skirts must cover the knees.

In the colonnade at the right side of St. Peter's Square I saw a young man getting out of his blue jeans and remaining in his underpants so that he could lend his trousers to a miniskirted girl. After she had been barred from St. Peter's the couple had evidently decided to visit the basilica separately, on one pair of pants. The halberded Swiss Guard at the Bronze Door a few steps up from the colonnade watched the strip scene with a poker face.

• Us Others •

JULY 23

Four youths in medieval costumes rowed a barge down the Tiber last night; in it stood a burly man dressed up as "Captain of the

People" carrying the purple banner of the Trastevere district. Floodlights lent by the army illuminated the river scene, the band of the municipal police played popular tunes, the crowds ashore cheered, and torches were burning in the narrow right-bank streets. Such was the start of this year's Festa di Noantri, which in Trastevere's own special dialect means "Feast of us others."

The *trasteverini* have always maintained they are different from other people in the city and claimed to be the sole direct descendants of the ancient Romans. Actually, the neighborhood between the west bank of the Tiber and the slope of the Janiculum was in antiquity and in the Middle Ages a suburb where many Jews and other immigrants lived. For the last several centuries before the 1970s, Trastevere was a working-class section.

Its populace has for many years celebrated its supposed distinctness from the rest of the Romans with a festival at the height of summer, featuring lots of wine drunk at the tables that spilled from the taverns into the piazzas and the sidewalk-less lanes; cold meat cut from roast suckling pigs; nostalgic and bawdy songs; and fireworks. One major attraction was the Trastevere belles, voluptuous-looking young women who habitually wore disdainful expressions and were jealously guarded by brothers, boyfriends, and husbands. During my first summers in the city I never missed the Noantri fun.

Then gentrification began. Now it is very fashionable to live in once-proletarian Trastevere; many of the new residents are affluent, pay high rents, and patronize the new restaurants and nightspots. The old Festa di Noantri has become a two-week revival folklore happening with street theater by professional troupes and revelry organized by travel agents. It won't be easy during the coming nights to find some sleep in the neighborhood's sophisticated, reconverted lofts before two or three A.M.

• Alfresco Opera •

Last night's premiere of an outdoor production of Verdi's *Rigoletto* by the Rome Opera House in the Piazza di Siena was creditable, although the stripped-down building-block stage sets disappointed the Canadian tourists seated next to me; they had expected visual lavishness. I didn't know what to make of the voices, which the electronic amplification system seemed to distort. I liked the Bulgarian soprano Darina Takova as Gilda, though. The orchestra of the Teatro dell'Opera played the familiar score competently enough under Maestro Paolo Carignani, the night was balmy and the sky starry, and the pine trees surrounding the square in the Villa Borghese gardens lent a note of solemnity.

Rome, in sum, again has open-air opera after last summer's silence and the strident wrangling between the ever-militant seven operatic unions and City Hall. I passed up *Tosca*, with which the current seven-week season started earlier this month, because I had seen too many top-class productions of Puccini's Roman classic over the years (one with the legendary Maria Jeritza), and didn't want to be disappointed.

This year's outdoor season in the Villa Borghese gardens was modest compared with the operatic splendor in the Baths of Caracalla during many summers between the 1930s and 1993. A spectacular *Aïda* with live horses and mules, some years even with elephants, on the huge stage used to be a crowd pleaser and tourist magnet. During the performances, sanitation workers disguised as Ethiopian slaves wielding brooms moved onstage in ballet steps to clean up after the animals, while the orchestra and singers went on with Verdi's triumphal music. No *Aïda* this summer!

Last year the state authorities, at the behest of archeologists, vetoed any further use of the imposing Caracalla ruins for shows, and Rome that summer remained without alfresco opera, to the regret of tourists.

The city has meanwhile decided to adapt an area behind the Caracalla Baths, close to the 1,700-year-old Aurelian Walls, as a new site for the open-air performances. It's hoped there will also be stables for the animals starring in *Aïda*.

August

• Hallowed Holiday •

A few days ago Pope John Paul II said he was praying "for all those who for various reasons, not excluding sickness, are forced to remain in the city" this time of the year. The pontiff, just back from a ten-day alpine vacation in the Val d'Aosta in Italy's northwest, was addressing pilgrims at Castelgandolfo, his airy summer residence.

John Paul II's words echoed the conviction shared by almost everybody here that it's a disgrace to stay in Rome in August. Only a small minority actually likes the city during this period.

Rome has progressively emptied the last two weeks, and since last Friday is nearly deserted. Ferragosto, the Italians' hallowed mid-August festival, this year fell on a Tuesday, and many of those who held out in the city until the preceding weekend won't be back before next Monday at the earliest.

The Italian word *Ferragosto* contains the Latin root for "vacation" and the name of Emperor Augustus, who first introduced the holiday as a populist gesture. Even slaves could take it easy during the dog days. The Roman Catholic Church implanted its own celebration, the feast of the Virgin Mary's Ascension to Heaven, on the ineradicable festival, and for the Italian state it is of course a legal day of rest. I made my own espresso because I was sure I wouldn't find one open coffee bar today, yet a couple of them were doing business around the Vatican, catering almost exclusively to tourists. A Carabinieri sergeant on duty near St. Peter's Square told me: "No vacation for us today. All our men are alerted, and all our squad cars are in service. You know, the thieves and robbers don't take off *Ferragosto*."

• A Homecoming of Sorts •

AUGUST 29

City Hall stated yesterday that the rehabilitation of the Piazza Vittorio was completed. I know *that* square because it is in the long-scruffy neighborhood where I lived for two years when I first moved to Rome.

Officially it is the Piazza Vittorio Emanuele II, but most Romans are at a loss if you refer to the square by its full name. Everybody says "Piazza Vittorio" and, calling it that way, hardly anybody will think of bearded, womanizing King Victor Emmanuel II (1820–78), the ruler of Piedmont-Sardinia who became the first sovereign of unified Italy.

The Piazza Vittorio is the center of a section that sprang up after 1870, when Rome had been designated as the nation's capital, and needed plenty of new housing for the bureaucrats and professional people who poured in from Piedmont and other northern regions. Their idiom and manners were alien to the easygoing Romans, who reacted to the newcomers with disdain and called them *buzzurri,* a dialect word still in use to denote primitive provincials.

New city quarters were quickly developed for the northern Italian immigrants amid the bankruptcy and corruption scandals that often accompany building booms. Those late-nineteenth-century neighborhoods in various parts of the city are at once recognizable by their rectilinear streets and geometrical squares; their architecture, known as *stile umbertino* (Humbert style), is the eclecticism marking the era of King Humbert, who reigned from 1878 until his assassination by an anarchist in 1900. Some Humbertine districts around town are reasonably well maintained or even look prosperous; the streets around Piazza Vittorio aren't and don't.

Few tourists ever see the Piazza Vittorio and the surrounding residential blocks, although they are close to the splendid Basilica of Saint Mary Major (Santa Maria Maggiore), the world's largest church dedicated to the Virgin Mary, and not too far from the Lateran. Many Romans living elsewhere in the city, however, make periodic shopping expeditions to the seedy neighborhood because the big outdoor food market in the Piazza Vittorio is reputed to have the lowest prices in town and a vast selection of fresh produce.

Since the early 1980s the renowned market can also be reached by the B line of the subway; in fact, the entire subway system is steered and monitored by a control center adjacent to the station deep below the piazza. The station signs read VITTORIO EMANUELE, but for everybody it's still Piazza Vittorio. Long underground passages lead to exits at the various sides of the square.

"At night those long corridors are scary," said the woman news vendor near the east exit. The rectangular square is bordered on all four sides by arcaded buildings that must have looked stately at the time of King Humbert and now are shabby.

I hadn't revisited the Piazza Vittorio for five or six years and found it tidied up. The tracks of the Nos. 14, 516, and 517 tram lines had been shifted to the east side, and new shrubbery had been planted in the park in the square's center. That park is a late descendant of the lush gardens of Gaius Maecenas, the rich friend of Emperor Augustus and patron of Horace and Virgil, which extended to that spot. The so-called Magic Door opposite a fountain in the park is a chunk of masonry carrying cabalistic signs, maybe relating to alchemy; it too has been cleaned up.

Many buildings around the piazza, alas, have descended a few notches closer into slumdom since I had last seen them. Property owners and landlords have clearly decided there is no point in spending money on maintenance when multitudes of Third World immigrants, legal and illegal, will pay good rent for any place they can move into, run-down though it may be. "A dozen *negri* [Negroes] will sleep in a small room, sometime in shifts," the woman at the newsstand told me. She sounded neither contemptuous nor compassionate, just matter-of-fact.

The graffiti on houses and the posters under the arcades were in Arabic or Indian script. The Piazza Vittorio section, southwest of the broad bundle of railroad tracks that lead into the Stazione Termini, the central terminal, has been filling up during the last few decades with Africans, Asians, and Latin Americans. On a street corner just off the Piazza Vittorio there is now a big Chinese grocery that I haven't seen before.

From the newsstand where I bought a daily I turned left into one of the streets running from the Piazza Vittorio to the railroad tracks, the Via Ricasoli. It looks mean now, but it still stirs memories I wouldn't miss.

In the spring of 1938 I had written to a friend in Rome, asking her to find me a very cheap room. At that time I didn't know how I would be able to pay for even the most Spartan accommodation. Hitler's army had just invaded Austria, and I was allowed to take with me no more than ten marks (German currency had been introduced at once) on leaving what had become Greater Germany as a voluntary exile.

My friend met me at the old Stazione Termini and took me to a walkup at 16 Via Ricasoli. After twenty-six hours—the Vienna-Rome trip had taken that long—in a second-class coach I was too tired to investigate the surroundings in which I would start my new Roman life. I had been a tourist in the Italian capital before, but the neighborhood where I found myself was completely new to me.

I had a small room with an iron bed frame and coarse but clean linen, with little else in the way of furniture. I was in one of the two apartments left and right of the sixth-floor landing that formed a modest *pensione*. The middle-aged, raven-haired landlady who had traces of a mustache welcomed me with a warmth that astonished me, and half an hour later I was asleep.

Protracted din that became louder by the minute awakened me at what seemed to me the middle of the night but was actually about six A.M. I went to the window in my room to see what the racket was about, and found that the Via Ricasoli on the street level was lined with storage spaces. Yelling and laughing, a bunch of men were noisily opening shutters and pulling out carts loaded with sawhorses, boards, crates, and balances for market stands. The market itself, I realized, was under the palm trees on the square a few yards to the right of me. That was the first I saw of the Piazza Vittorio.

The noise in the Via Ricasoli most of the day was remarkable. The shouts of market vendors were heard all morning. In the early afternoon, Monday to Saturday, sanitation men arrived in force, shouting and singing, put the garbage into metal containers that were rumorously emptied into a truck, and then hosed down the market area and the approaches to it. Our neighborhood smelled of disinfectant for the rest of the day.

That fall and winter we who lived near the market had to get used to a new acoustic treat afternoons and evenings until late, Sundays included. A modest carnival had been permitted to put up its rides and tents in the unkempt Piazza Vittorio park, and the mechanical organ that was part of a merry-go-round blared a song, always the same, for many hours. I still have it in my ears and caught myself humming it in the square today.

Our *pensione* wasn't the quietest place, either. Signora Virginia, our landlady who had come from an olive-growing village in the Sabine Hills north of Rome, chanted with the radio in her kitchen that kept pouring out pop numbers, talked loudly with her lodgers, yelled at her two teenage children, and boisterously joked with her frequent visitors, who would roar with laughter. The espresso she brewed all the time was one of the reasons why she was so popular with her friends. I, too, soon became a regular in her kitchen.

Signora Virginia's husband was rarely seen, and when he was he didn't have much to say. He hailed from her village, was much older than she, and was a cop. When Hitler was about to undertake a state visit to Rome in May 1938 the policeman took me and the other foreigner among the lodgers—Ernest Nansen, formerly Ernst Nathanson of Berlin—aside and told us that hundreds of Jews and other émigrés from Germany and Austria had been taken into "protective custody" for the duration of the Führer's presence in Italy, but that he had guaranteed to his superiors that the two of us wouldn't attempt any nonsense; "just don't go out during the next few days."

Thus we were under house arrest. Had we violated his trust, signora Virginia's husband probably wouldn't have reported us, but the authorities would have known all the same because the janitor who sat in his little booth in the dingy ground-floor hall all day was a Fascist Party informer, as I was to find out years later.

Signor Ernesto, as we called Mr. Nansen, had been an editor at one of Berlin's big newspapers and had emigrated soon after Hitler came to power; his Lutheran wife went with him. He had landed a translator's job at the *Giornale d'Italia,* the Roman afternoon newspaper that was then a mouthpiece of the Fascist foreign policy. Nansen and I became friends. When the German refugee came home from his office with the first edition of his paper we sat down to coffeee, and the former editor analyzed the contents of the *Giornale d'Italia* for my benefit; I learned a lot from him. Following Mussolini's infamous racial laws the Nansens emigrated again, this time to Canada. I never heard of them again, but when a son was born to us we named him Ernesto after the bespectacled, erudite Berliner with his invincible sense of humor.

Signora Virginia had a second Jewish family among her lodgers. They were an Italian who worked as a salesman at the La Rinascente department store, his fragile-looking wife, and their blond three-year-old boy, Leo. They lived in a cramped room that wasn't bigger than ours. I grew fond of Leo, who had the run of the *pensione* and visited me in our room from time to time. He called me "Pavolo" instead of Paolo, the Italian form of my first name, and since Pavolo rhymes with *cavolo* (cabbage), which is also a euphemism for a rude Italian word, little Leo caused a lot of hilarity.

We had long moved to a comfortable apartment near the Vatican when my wife, in my absence, got an anguished call from signora Virginia: "I can't talk, but come and see me!" They met and our former landlady tearfully told my wife that Leo's father had come home from work one evening and found the room empty. The Nazis who were then occupying Rome had come earlier that day and taken little Leo and his mother away; they vanished without a trace. Whenever I hear the word *Holocaust* I first think of the small blond child Leo.

A few years ago the Via Ricasoli was in the news: a large part of the front wall, about half of the entire facade, had crashed into the street, apparently without any warning. Some people were injured and all inhabitants of the building had to be evacuated. Signora Virginia and her family had long moved elsewhere; over the years I had learned that her son had become a bank official and her daughter a nurse. Today I saw that No. 16 has been completely repaired. One of the storerooms on the street level has been converted into a Bengali club, but the others are still used as overnight shelters for market paraphernalia.

I wandered past the market stands. The crowd of shoppers was as thick as I remembered it from old times, and much more picturesque. There were African and Asian women, some in white or flowery dress, others in blue jeans, many with children. A cute little girl, maybe an Eritrean or Somali, said to a tall black woman "*Mamma, gelato!*" in a genuine Roman cadence. Near the food section a line of Senegalese were offering pots and pans, crockery, sunglasses, leatherware, and perfumes.

August

At what once was my favorite espresso bar, on the south side of the piazza, I had a cappuccino. Two youngsters had soft drinks and spoke in what I thought was Albanian. Then I heard them pronounce the words *Lazio* and *Roma;* they are discussing soccer. Another pair of neo-Romans.

Index

Index

Index

Index

Index

Index

Index

Index

Index